JOHN
WESLEY

Founder of the Methodist Church

Sam Wellman

BARBOUR
PUBLISHING, INC.
Uhrichsville, Ohio

Other books in the "Heroes of the Faith" series:

Brother Andrew

Gladys Aylward

William and Catherine Booth

John Bunyan

William Carey

Amy Carmichael

George Washington Carver

Fanny Crosby

Frederick Douglass

Jonathan Edwards

Jim Elliot

Charles Finney

Billy Graham

C. S. Lewis

Eric Liddell

David Livingstone

Martin Luther

D. L. Moody

Samuel Morris

George Müller

Watchman Nee

John Newton

Florence Nightingale

Mary Slessor

Charles Spurgeon

Hudson Taylor

Corrie ten Boom

Mother Teresa

Sojourner Truth

©MCMXCVII by Sam Wellman

ISBN 1-55748-978-5

Published by Barbour Publishing, Inc., P.O. Box 719, Uhrichsville, OH 44683
http://www.barbourbooks.com

Cover illustration ©Dick Bobnick

Member of the
Evangelical Christian
Publishers Association

Printed in the United States of America.

JOHN WESLEY

In memory of Ack Reinhold, Mike Reinhold, and Steve McKee.

When duty whispers low, "You must."
Youth answers, "I can."

(from Emerson)

one

The Young Boy

"At last," John murmured happily.

The moment the nursemaid finished wiping John's face, he slipped not inside the curtain that surrounded the bed where he and baby brother Charles slept, but into the hall from the nursery. The nursemaid would never notice John was not in bed with babbly Charles. She was too busy washing John's sisters Patty, then Anne, then Hetty, then Molly. By the time they were all ready for bed, John would be back. He had done this for several nights now.

John tiptoed down the hall toward a voice. It was sister Emily saying, "If I can get a decent wardrobe, I know I can go to a manor house as a governess. . . ."

"And you'll meet a fine young gentleman, for sure," gushed sister Sukey.

John quietly entered the bedroom shared by his oldest sisters Emily and Sukey. In amber lantern light they brushed each other's hair every evening, all the while staring at each other in a mirror and sharing stories. John slipped down behind the bed, out of sight.

"Surely father can spare a few pennies for me," Emily grumbled, "if he can send Sammy to London to a fine school like Westminster."

"Oh, surely," Sukey agreed. "How much money do you think Father makes as rector of Epworth?"

"I don't speculate how much he makes," Emily sniffed curtly.

"Oh, I'm sorry. . . ."

"I know how much he makes," Emily giggled, enjoying the joke on her younger sister.

"You devil!" Sukey laughed. John heard her gently slap Emily on the shoulder. "How much then?"

"One hundred and thirty pounds a year!"

"My! So much! And doesn't Uncle Jack pay him for his couplets?"

"Once upon a time." Resentment thinned Emily's voice. Every night their father sat in his study downstairs for hours composing poetry, some of which had appeared in their Uncle Jack Dunton's magazine *Athenian Gazette*—before it was discontinued. Outside Greek and Hebrew lessons, the children at home—six daughters and two brothers—rarely talked to their father at all, except for his pet, Hetty.

John bathed in the golden silence. It was wonderful when his sisters talked and it was wonderful when they didn't talk. When they didn't talk, he had time to chew on what they had already said. For instance, he just realized with a shock that his sisters, when they were alone, did not address each other "Sister This" and "Sister That." They were supposed to always do that! And what was that Emily just said? Had she talked casually with one of the servants? That wasn't allowed, either. Should he scold them? The urge was overpowering.

He stood up. "Sister Emily. Sister Sukey. Pray, let me remind you that you are not supposed—"

"Master John Wesley!" A hand crunched his shoulder.

"Mother!"

"What are you doing in here?" she demanded.

"Listening, Mother."

His mother's frown tripled. All three towered over him

8

now. "Bend over that bed," his mother said. "Give me your brush, Miss Emily."

John rose and bent over the bed, knowing all too well what was next. But how many? One? Five? Ten? He felt the dull pain once, twice, three times. The spanking was over, but not the pain. The pain would rise from a dull aching bass to a stinging chorus of sopranos. Yes, the pain was climbing higher and higher, but a complaint would bring more pain. He gritted his teeth. . . .

"And me with child." His mother sounded winded. "If you can't be trusted to say your prayers in your room, Master John, you will do them for me right now. Stand up!"

John recited the Lord's Prayer. He could not remember ever not knowing it. Then he said a prayer for Mother and Father. Those prayers were easy to remember. It was a good thing, too, because pain prickled his bottom.

"Finish this article, Master John: 'No man's will is forced. . . .'"

John gulped and finished it: " '. . . . His sin is his own.' "

"That seems particularly appropriate tonight! Now recite some Scripture, Master John."

" 'Honor your father and your mother, as the Lord your God has commanded you,' " he said brightly.

"Now off to bed, sir!"

Sometimes even inside the rectory John could feel that cold, wet expanse of lowlands called the Fens. From the height of the second-floor nursery the cold, dank pools of water and canals stretched as far as his eyes could see.

This February night of 1709 was such a shivery night. He trembled. So what he had done for several nights was wrong, a sin. It didn't seem so. He had learned a lot from his older sisters, especially Emily—maybe as much as he did the rest of the day. In spite of the sleep that tugged at him, he dwelt on how he spent every day.

Every minute of every day was planned in this Wesley family. Each day John arose only when approved by the nursemaid, then said the Lord's Prayer, then prayed for his family, then recited a collect from the *Book of Common Prayer,* then recited some Scripture, just as he did at night before bed. Then he dressed and hurried downstairs to breakfast. He sat at a small table with Charles, Patty and Anne. All the others sat at the large table. Father Samuel Wesley said grace until John's stomach growled. If John ate his portion and wanted something more, like bread, he silently motioned a maid over and whispered, "Pray give me bread, Madam." No one talked out loud at the table, unless asked to speak by Father or Mother.

After the meal, the toddlers Charles and Patty disappeared to the nursery and the rest of the children gathered in the parlor where Mother Susanna directed their studies. Like every Wesley child before him, John had been reading since his fifth birthday. Only Holy Scripture was suitable for learning to read. He began his first few stumbling words in Genesis and now was crawling though Leviticus. At noon they stopped studying to eat lunch and rest. Then from two to five they studied again. As they grew older, their studies expanded into Hebrew and Greek with father in the evenings. . . .

"But now it's Latin and math and geography and history," John muttered into the darkness.

Poetry and music were not neglected. No child of this Wesley family was considered educated who could not only read and write poetry, but read and compose music as well. An educated person could discuss a sonnet or a sonata as easily as the weather. Father Samuel not only wrote couplets, but composed hymns. His hymns were not part of the liturgy of the church; it was too rigid for anything new. But father found occasions for them.

For his own musical outlet, John was beginning to play the flute. Each day he felt more comfortable with its shrill piping.

Before supper, Susanna took one child aside for his or her own very special hour of instruction. John's hour was on Thursday. After supper, they retired to their rooms to be dressed in night robes and washed for bed by their nursemaid. Every moment of every day was intended for some good purpose.

John could see now he had sinned. He was tired, too. Rarely had he stayed awake so long. It must be guilt—yes, the devil himself—that robbed him of sleep this night. He lay in bed and kept thinking of how he had sinned. Perhaps the devil somehow had tempted John, but he had sinned of his own free will, just as the article so wisely stated. . . .

John awoke very tired. The curtains around the bed had the soft glow of dawn. But why was he so tired? Usually he couldn't wait to bounce out of bed.

He called to the nursemaid, "Pray, if it please you, Madam, I wish to arise now."

And where was babbly, happy Charles? This was most unusual. And where was the nursemaid? How long should John wait? He wished to look out of the curtains. But would that once again plunge him into sin?

He waited and felt a sense of dread. He called again. No answer. He heard a cacophony like ocean surf—but no, it was more like loud gabbling voices of demons. He had to look.

Flames danced across the ceiling! Was he dreaming of hell? He smelled smoke. . . .

"Fire!" he screamed, almost choking the words off in fear of sinning. "But I'm the only one in here. Where is everyone?"

He jumped from bed and ran across the room, which was

aglow with a hellish pink, to open the door. The hall was a red wall of flame.

"Trapped!" he screamed, and slammed the door shut.

John glanced around the room. Tiny licks of flame splashed from the walls. A window looked like an oasis.

"But it's too high!" he whined.

There was a dresser. He pulled out drawers and climbed them like a ladder, praying the dresser would not tip over. Now he reached the level of the window. Yes! In the flickering light of the inferno he saw faces down in the yard. Yes, there below were some of his sisters, huddled, frightened, their faces eerie orange.

He rested one knee on the window sill and hammered on the panes. His father appeared among his sisters, looking bewildered. John tried to open the window. It was stuck.

"Oh, please, Lord, let them see me," John whimpered.

two

Exposure to Commoners

"Look up here!" John screamed.

John's father Samuel scurried around below as if trying to account for everyone. Soon John saw eyes directed up at his window. Their faces were cast in blood-red horror. Yes, he was sure now they knew he had been left behind.

John hammered on the window. "Up here!" he screamed.

Two men broke loose from the crowd. They ran to a spot below John and disappeared. Suddenly a hand shoved his window open with shattering force. The hand reached in, clamped John's arm and yanked him out so hard his head snapped. He blacked out.

Moments later he opened his eyes. His head was spinning. Faces jumped before his eyes.

Did everyone get out of the inferno? Where was Mother? Where was Charles?

"Master John! Praise God." It was his mother's voice.

"Mother!" John looked into his mother's frightened face, smudged black. "Where is Charles?"

"He is safe. Everyone got out. Praise God. You're alive." She cried and hugged him. He could tell she had thought he was lost.

John noticed his father staring at him, loose-jawed. His face seemed in awe. "John is a brand plucked out of the burning," he said in amazement.

The wind blew the flames into a raging torch, so fiery the people had to move away. And yet as they watched with hot, flushed faces, the icy wind of the watery Fens bit at their backs.

Soon John was with his sisters and brother across the village square in Saint Andrew's Church, where his father conducted services. All were wrapped in blankets. His mother and the servants were there, too. The nursemaid was trembling.

"I'm sorry, Master John," the nursemaid whispered. "I grabbed the babies, Charles and Patty, and called for the rest of you to follow. We had to run down the stairs through flames. Then outside I saw you were not with us. Oh, God, I thought you were lost."

"But I'm here, 'plucked out of the burning.' Pray, do not distress yourself. Praise God."

After a while Samuel came in. He seemed bewildered. "Burned to the ground," he muttered. "It was all timber and plaster and thatch."

"Not the dove coop!" John remembered suddenly.

"No, Master John," his father said softly. "The doves are safe. And the barn and stock survived, too." He sighed. "The foxes have holes and the birds of the air have nests, but the children of God have no place to lay their heads."

Samuel looked around and straightened to his full height. "We must find homes for the children as soon as possible."

Only Emily stayed with mother Susanna—to help with the baby who was due in just one month. All the others were dispersed. Hetty and Sukey went to London to stay with Uncle Matthew Wesley. The others went to live with neighbors around Epworth.

John's life was turned upside down. All order one day, and all disorder the next. He was supposed to be in his father's charge. Yet his father had little time for him. So John was left almost immediately with a farm family. And the grown-ups in that family introduced him almost immediately to their son Oliver, John's age but nearly a head taller.

When John realized the grown-ups were departing, he was shocked. His mother had forbidden him to play with the rough children of Epworth. He deliberated, then advised the adults, "Pray, good friends, I'm not allowed diversions among. . . ."

"They ain't listening," Oliver growled, interrupting him. "I hope you wasn't going to say you're too good for the likes of me. Come on outside."

Soon, John was alone with the boy in the barn. Oliver had been most deferential to John when the parents were there. Now his face reddened. "Well, if it ain't the little Wesley cherub hisself," Oliver snarled.

"Master Oliver, I'll not have you speak that way of the Lord's angels."

"You ain't going to do nothing about it. I'm a Fensman. I don't answer to God or queens or men."

"You will answer to God soon enough, if you don't answer to Queen Anne first!"

"Ain't you the talker!"

Oliver laughed, but John knew the threat in his voice was real. Even buffered by his close-knit family, John had heard the Fensmen were nasty. Some in the crowd around the fire that night were muttering that Fensmen started the fire. In the past, Fensmen had stabbed his father's cattle and sheep on the glebe, the land surrounding the rectory. They even had beaten up the family dog, a brave mastiff, sent out in the night after them. His father's public attacks on sinners were not appreciated. Nor were his visits appreciated where he privately admonished the Fensmen. John overheard his sisters say their father had been thrown in jail once because he

15

couldn't pay a debt. The Fensmen had cheered.

Oliver frowned. "Let's have a good look at you, Cherub Wesley. Ain't you twinkly-eyed, to be sure? A right pointy nose to poke into my business, too. I'll soon blunt that impertinence!"

An older boy, a farm worker in very dirty clothes, walked into the barn. He studied how the two younger boys stood face to face, hands on hips. Finally he said, "I don't want the destruction of that dainty little fellow on my conscience. So you take care of him, Oliver, or I'll take care of you."

John was shocked. How could a servant speak that way to Oliver? He had an overpowering urge to admonish him. "Sir, I pray believe you've stepped beyond the bounds of proper. . . ."

"Shut up!" snapped Oliver, angry over the warning from the older boy. "Come on with me, you little blighter."

During the next days John learned how small he really was. Oliver had friends. They, too, were taller than John. As a small boy among the small people in his large family, John had not known how small he was until now. He now realized, too, that his father was a head shorter than most grown men. And John now realized he must learn how to cope among the boys of the Fens, just as he had learned how to cope within his own family.

He was shoved and tripped and poked and harassed, but he bore it. Finally, the bigger boys grudgingly accepted him like a small, tag-along brother. They took little notice of him unless he pointed out some sin they had committed. And John did this often. He couldn't stop doing it, although it brought him pain every time. He seemed to sense he was a replica of his father among the Fensmen.

John learned much about the inflexible Fensmen. The draining of the swamps with canals enraged them. Years before, when all England was aflame with the Civil War, the Fensmen fought neither for Cromwell nor King Charles. They fought the Dutchmen imported by wealthy noblemen to drain the Fens. Their world was hard but precious. Paddling about in their skiffs, they harvested their bounty of fish and frogs and turtles and prawns in their snares and nets. The wet treasure of the Fens was theirs.

"It ain't going to be long before outsiders drain the life out of the Fens," Oliver complained bitterly. "Then the Fens ain't going to be good for nothing."

Every Sunday, John's father came for him. Each time they passed the quietly gliding Trent River, his father would recite a couplet he had composed about the river. Minutes later, John would be reunited for a few hours with his family in the great stone church of Saint Andrew.

John had a new red-cheeked baby sister, Kezzy, named after one of Job's daughters, Kezziah. From Hetty's whispers, John learned his father composed more than couplets; he also labored over some gigantic prose work about the suffering Job.

In Saint Andrew's, order once again reigned for John. His father did not deviate one iota from the service set down in the *Book of Common Prayer*. Then came the sermon. He blistered the parishioners for their slackness. The fire had not intimidated him one bit. It had only tempered his tongue into a harder thrust.

But back on the farm every Sunday afternoon, the Lord's Day was not observed, except for grumbling over the unnecessary hardness of the sermon. The Fens people worked and played as they would have any afternoon. And soon John became accustomed to talking to servants any time he felt like it, to playing games on the Lord's Day, to singing crude songs, to scuffling in the dirt, to yelling for more food and to speaking the coarse accent of the Fens.

He hardened under the soft exterior. He had been the victim of every prank known to the boys of the Fens. And still he politely pointed out their every sin, even though it was getting harder to remember just what was sinful and what was not.

Oliver shook his head in wonder. "You're stubborn enough to be one of the Fens, Cherub Wesley, except you're on the wrong side of almost every issue."

One year later, the entire Wesley family was reunited in the new rectory. John would miss the rough boys of the Fens. He knew he seldom would be able to talk to them now. Susanna would make sure of that.

It was odd how he missed them, considering the hard way they had teased him. But he had discovered things about himself. He was small, to be sure, but he had a tough hide. It seemed he could take any amount of teasing, and although he felt indignation during the teasing, he didn't carry any anger from it afterwards at all. It was as if he were remembering someone else being mistreated.

The new rectory was no building of plaster and wood and thatch this time. It was a handsome two-story building of red brick, roofed with tile. Light glittered off it from more than fifty windows. Three chimneys spoke of many cozy fireplaces. Inside the front door, a parlor yawned off to the left of the entrance hall. Back of it was an unseen dining room. To the right of the entrance hall was a large room that opened into the kitchen at the back of the house.

With little enthusiasm, Susanna explained, "The story above has the bedrooms and your father's study." She walked into the room at the right. "It took one year to rebuild the rectory." Her voice was now full of fire. "Only the Lord knows how long it will take me to rebuild you into children of God. This is the room where we will study."

And study they did. Finally, John pleased his mother again. He no longer spoke to servants unless it was a whispered request of some kind. He wouldn't dream of playing games on the Lord's Day. Crude songs were replaced by hymns. He lost every trace of the coarse accent of the Fens. But deep inside he carried bittersweet memories of the rough commoners, untouched by loyalty to the Crown, unmoved by the liturgy of the Church of England, only confused and hardened by their life of toil. So perhaps the fire had worked some small miracle in him.

He was sensitive to undercurrents of discontent now. All was not well within the Wesley family, especially among his sisters, and most of all with Emily. One Saturday evening when mother Susanna was with Charles giving him his special hour of instruction, John, now eight, approached Emily. As usual, Sukey was with her.

"Pray, Sister Emily, tell me what bothers you."

Emily glanced at Sukey. "Nothing bothers me."

He winced at her lack of "Brother John," but bit his tongue. "Pray, Sister Emily, I only want to help. Trust me that I won't tell your confidence to mother or father."

Emily's jaw dropped. "I believe he really wouldn't."

"Oh, tell him then," Sukey said. "Besides, why should we protect him? Doesn't he get enough privileges?"

"Pray, Sister Sukey, allow me to disagree," John said. "It's common knowledge Mother works me hardest of all."

"And why is that?" Sukey barked. "Because you will leave in a few short years to go to public school. She has to make sure the coarseness of the Fens no longer shows. You mustn't embarrass the godly Wesleys. That's why."

John winced again. "But, Sisters Emily and Sukey, you both seem uncommonly bitter."

Emily scowled. "Father owes four hundred pounds for rebuilding the rectory. He couldn't manage to make ends meet before the fire; how do you think he will manage now—hundreds of pounds in debt? And we still have almost no furniture!"

"Then, Sister Emily, I won't go to public school."

"Of course you will," she snapped bitterly. "It will just mean we girls must do with less!"

"But surely, Sister Emily—"

"Oh, bother with that 'sister' bit! I'm twenty years old. Just one year younger than Sammy who is now studying at Oxford! And what future do I have, knowing how to read English, Hebrew, Latin and Greek as well as Sammy does? I'll tell you, Master John. If there is ever enough money left over—after father's mastiff and horse are well fed, of course—father may buy me a plain dress so I can use my education as a governess!"

John said weakly, "But surely, Sister Emily, no one reads John Milton as well as you. . . ."

Emily growled, "By the time Sammy leaves Oxford you will be attending public school. By the time you leave public school for Oxford Charles will be in public school. By the time you leave Oxford Charles will be ready for Oxford. Do you know how old I'll be before Charles leaves Oxford?"

"No, Sister Emily."

"Almost forty!" she screamed. "Sukey will be thirty-six!"

"But, Sister Emily, won't you marry a fine—"

"Around here? Look around you at the coarse farmers and merchants. And do we get visitors from other parts of England? Hardly. Unless they have gills and fins. Even Sammy can't get his fine-bred Oxford friends to come here to visit. If father had sent me to London with Hetty and Sukey maybe I could have met a real gentleman."

20

Emily could not be consoled. All his life John had thought his sisters at a certain age would find suitable husbands and live happily ever after. What had happened? Was it his parents' fault? Was it the knowledge they imparted to their daughters that made them so discontent? Or was it the way the daughters were kept from the commoners so that they were repelled by them? And why did they blame their father for everything?

In the next days he discretely talked with fifteen-year-old Molly, fourteen-year-old Hetty and nine-year-old Anne. They, too, were inconsolable.

The discontent was not pervasive among his sisters. Five-year-old Patty and the toddler Kezzy were as yet oblivious to their miserable fates, but they would learn from their unhappy sisters soon enough.

Four-year-old Charles knew nothing of what was going on. John never confided in him. Charles was not like John at all. Whereas John was quiet and serious, Charles hummed tunes and enjoyed himself. John was even-tempered, but Charles could explode in anger, then chatter happily a few seconds later. It dawned on John that he was serious and rational—like his mother Susanna. Charles seemed artistic and hot-tempered like his father Samuel. In any event, Charles couldn't even read yet; he seemed a baby to John.

John tried to sympathize with his sisters. Yes, it was disappointing to be educated and expect so little from it, he told them. But the very shelter that protected them warped their perspective. John had seen the dirty-faced, red-knuckled women who lived on farms in the Fens. His sisters knew nothing of really hard life. And then there were all their own dear Wesley brothers and sisters moldering under stones in the Epworth churchyard. Six of them. It was heartbreaking. Pink nubbins turning to soil! And they were not the only ones. Three more babies were buried over in a place called South Ormsby. The poor babies were all alone in some churchyard he had never seen. Yes, that was hard.

"Praise God for life," John told his five older sisters.

"Easy for you to say," Emily grumbled. "You'll soon be off to London, my little squire."

three

Formal Education

*I*t was a chilly January day in 1714 when ten-year-old John Wesley, in black broadcloth robe and knee pants, stepped off the stagecoach from Epworth. Charterhouse School was situated near Old Street and Aldersgate roads in London, far north of the Thames River, said Brother Sammy, who had met John and helped him carry his baggage inside. Towering Sammy was gruff with the boys in the dormitory and John guessed it was for his own protection, as if to warn them Big Brother just might come back. For Sammy knew very well what was coming.

It wasn't long in coming, either.

That night John's bed was short-sheeted. "A most excellent trick indeed," John said as good-naturedly as he could while wearily remaking the bed. Anger was like fuel to pranksters. The boys of the Fens had prepared him well for this test. He must not only be unflappable, but delight in the mischief.

The next morning he found his knee pants tied in knots. "How amusing," John chirped merrily as he wrestled the knots loose.

By the time he ran three laps around the courtyard and washed up in the cloister next to the yard, he was very late for prayers in the chapel. During Latin prayers, the boys next to John feigned getting up and down again and again to lure John into a mistake. His heart was beating hard. There seemed not a moment of tranquillity.

"Just why were you so late to chapel?" asked a scowling schoolmaster named Thomas Walker after prayers.

"I ran laps around the courtyard for my health, as I promised my father."

The schoolmaster was speechless.

At breakfast, John was summoned to the headmaster, Dr. Thomas Burnet. The aged headmaster had no idea what John was talking about. His milky eyes were vacant. When John returned to his table, his plate was empty. The bread and slice of cheese were gone. He forced a smile of appreciation for the trick. During Greek grammar, several boys coughed and sneezed and snorted as he recited. John smiled at their rudeness.

His initiation continued in this petty vein for several days. Always John reminded himself to act good-natured and most polite. He would give the boys no delight in their mischief.

"So you're the new ward?" one of the older boys asked contemptuously, then added in mock pity, "The poorest of the poor. . . ."

"I was appointed by the Duke of Buckingham, sir," John replied.

"Don't put on airs for me," answered the older boy. "I'm in the same rotten ship as you. This Charterhouse School is expressly to help the sons of parents whose means are not sufficient for an education in keeping with their positions. And you are one of the few who pay not one farthing, beggar Wesley. I would say that makes you the poorest of the poor."

John had to admit he was right.

It wasn't what he expected of a boys' public school. There were forty boys at Charterhouse, but there were also eighty elderly men. Apparently, founder John Sutton had left money for both a boys' school and a center for the care of elderly men. The sight of decrepit men shuffling about the halls certainly added a solemn air. These ancient men had stories of the old times, stories John had never heard from his grandfathers, who died long before he was born.

"Some are so old they fought in England's bloody Civil War," John marveled.

Life became almost normal after a couple of weeks, if one could regard speaking Latin all day as normal. But John was quick with his studies. He soon justified his sponsorship to Charterhouse by the Duke of Buckingham. He quickly blended in with all the younger boys. He served the older boys no more or no less. He polished shoes, made their beds and ran risky errands. Many a time he slipped from Charterhouse to race madly to Smithfield Market to retrieve some drink or snack.

"Your reward is continued life, worm Wesley," sneered the older boy as John ran in, panting.

Enslaving younger boys was not all bad. Only the most sniveling boy didn't relish the future that promised he would be the slave master. And John was no exception. Why should he question the fairness of it? After all, Sammy had survived this public school ritual at Westminster, and he turned out all right. He appreciated it so much he was now an usher at Westminster. So why should John complain?

Sammy was kind and righteous. His wife was snippy, to be sure, when John corrected her. But she treated John all right, usually.

So the year passed. Aged Dr. Burnet died, to be replaced by a man John saw just as seldom. The schoolmaster Thomas Walker was John's mentor.

John rarely went home. More than ever, he now realized how isolated Epworth was. It might as well have been the Isle of Wight the way people talked about it. And the truth was that there were many weeks when one could not reach Epworth on horseback or by stagecoach. It could be reached only by boat. John remembered now how often his father slogged about the parish, drenched to the skin. John had thought nothing of that at the time. The way his older sisters talked, one would have thought his father was cozy in his study all the time, composing couplets. But now John knew they were wrong. Pastoring the Fens was a very hard life. So what if his father spent a few hours in the evening warming his bones and writing couplets? Wasn't John now writing Latin verse?

"And isn't that occupation enthralling?" he asked himself. "And don't the masters think I'm brisk at verse?"

But John sympathized more with his sisters now, too. His sensitivity seemed heightened after he had been at Charterhouse a couple of years. And with it came the presence of God. More than ever before in his life, he felt the presence of something beyond the detection of all senses. His curiosity, demanding reasonable answers for everything, had been a family joke. His father teased that even a "call of nature" could not rush John until he had reasoned it out first. But now John's mind fathomed God's presence.

What triggered this new sensation, this awareness of God? His readings of the Greek Testament? His prayers morning and night? His loneliness? In a moment of pure light, he realized it was the self-assurance that he was saved.

His own theology was far simpler than the complicated rhetoric of the clerics. Somehow, all thirty-nine articles of the Anglican faith had become distilled into: 1) one must not be bad to other people; 2) one must have a good attitude toward religion and 3) one must read the Bible, go to church and say prayers.

"Those three simple maxims make certain the reward of

eternity with the Father and the Heavenly Host," he explained confidently to younger boys.

But when he told Sammy that, Sammy just shrugged. "You're still very young, Brother."

John heard few complaints from his sisters at Epworth. Writing of their bitterness was not a step they wished to take with a boy John's age. They gently chided him for not writing more. Their main topic of note was the astonishing report the rectory was haunted! How odd, John thought, that even as he seemed coupled with the Holy Spirit now, the rectory could be invaded by an unwelcome spirit. The stories they wrote of the spirit staggered John. All in all, he was glad he was not back at Epworth. The stories defied reason.

The haunting started in December 1716. Some nights, the family heard knocking noises, then groans, finally the unmistakable sound of breaking bottles. The Wesleys' courageous mastiff only whimpered. Other nights, the family heard coins jangling and other noises.

The haunting became so familiar the family gave their ghost a name. "Old Jeffrey," John chuckled as he read his mother's letter.

His family's lack of fear calmed John. The noises were suspiciously juvenile. There were no lack of culprits who might have perpetrated such tricks. The family had just hired two new servants who may not have appreciated Samuel's outspoken devotion to their new sovereign. King George was a German of the House of Hanover who couldn't even speak English.

The servants were not the only suspects. John knew one of his discontented sisters might have enjoyed such tricks. Brother Charles had just left for Westminster; might not that additional example of special masculine privilege cause a small rebellion? Hetty was now twenty and particularly troublesome, according to Charles. The fact that she was the only one who would not talk about the haunting was certainly suspicious. But it didn't have to be one sister; it might be several in concert, enjoying their prank on Father immensely.

"On the other hand, Mother Susanna, a most critical observer, seems to believe the haunting is real," John said as he read one of her letters.

John himself had felt the presence of God—before the haunting ever happened. Might not Satan or one of his minions make their presence known, too? And might not the fallen one want to become a source of gentle amusement? If one thought all spirits were friendly or laughable, might not hell loose its horror?

John turned it over and over in his mind. Ghost stories were common in England, and John had learned to scoff as well as anyone, but now it had struck home. Satan would relish the role of a harmless buffoon.

"And the infernal haunting only pulls me away from my Hebrew," he reprimanded himself. And he would force himself back to work again.

John was absorbed in getting to the university at Oxford, as his father and his brother Sammy had done. At Charterhouse, John was too busy studying to indulge in an older boy's privileges over the younger. If he was not at Charterhouse, he was visiting at Westminster so Sammy could tutor him. Charles was living with Sammy, but John's visits were not social. Besides, John still considered Charles a pampered child.

Sammy worked John hard in Hebrew. It was Sammy who would decide when John was ready for Oxford.

Finally, in 1720, at seventeen, John left Charterhouse, schooled in the classics and every prank known to boys. Still held over from Epworth were his mother's critical eye and his father's outspoken righteousness and love of sovereigns. John arrived in the town of Oxford, about sixty miles west of Charterhouse School in London. England's other great university, Cambridge, lay about the same distance to the north of London.

Oxford dazzled John. "The golden stone spires and quadrangles seem paradise," he gushed.

The towering steeple of his own college, Christ Church, overwhelmed him, as did its immense quadrangle and the fan-vaulted ceiling of the Great Hall. The deanery of Christ Church had been the headquarters of King Charles the First during the bloody Civil War. The densest newcomer had to know all this grandeur and history signaled a great change in his life.

With the guidance of a tutor, John continued studying the Bible and classical literature in three languages besides English. He was such a correspondent now he spent nearly one day a week writing letters. The rest of the time he debated other students, composed poems, read the assigned studies and discussed what he read.

His reading was prodigious. He never wasted a moment. He went far beyond the assigned studies; he felt he had to. Books held the key to understanding the current state of mankind. In a year's time he would plow through the heavy Latin classics of Horace, Juvenal, Virgil and Cicero. He read ponderous religious tracts that covered the spectrum from stout defenses of the Church of England by John Ellis to fiery defenses of the true Gospel by dissidents like John Bunyan. He read plays, satires and farces. He read the erotic poems of John Donne; he read the pious poems of John Donne. He read the inspired poetry of George Herbert and John Milton.

"You can't possibly digest such a reading list," objected one opponent during a debate.

And many did claim his knowledge was superficial, but he seemed to be able to hold his own against the brightest scholars around. John suspected sour grapes from many of his detractors. "I've also read of the fox in Aesop's Fables," he replied with his usual calmness.

Occasionally, smallpox would break out. In the 1700s it was becoming the dread disease of England, as the plague had been the previous century. John already had survived smallpox, too young to know his life had hung by a thread. Now he had the comfort of knowing he could not get it again. But others dear to him were in jeopardy.

In 1723, smallpox broke out at both Epworth and Oxford. The disease felled a student in a room very near John's. The youth was bed-ridden by a high fever. In three days an angry rash flared on his face and palms and the soles of his feet. Two days later he was dead. His infection was so violent the disease never had a chance to run its course. Usually, the rash developed into pimples, which crusted. If the victim survived, he was often badly scarred.

Smallpox was very contagious. John was overjoyed to hear no one in the rectory at Epworth had succumbed to the disease.

A new method of prevention called "inoculation" was being tried in England. "But it is not widely available," reasoned the ever critical John. "And how effective will it be? Don't we need tests?"

After the first few years, many assigned studies disgusted him as superficial and utterly useless. He loved to read, but he did not read just to be reading.

"What is the reason for reading this?" he would lament to other students. "It serves no known purpose under the sun."

While the intellectual life of the undergraduates was heated and sometimes petty or downright useless, their social life was degenerate. Brother Sammy had warned John that morality at Oxford was on the decline. Sammy claimed this was true of the Church of England, too, under the guise that sin was not society's main problem. John's father Samuel agreed that backsliding had occurred ever since King Charles the Second had initiated the "Restoration" after the Civil War. England was immersed in an era when clerics focused on social ills, not sin.

Besides, serving the Lord must be practical for men, not a burden, said the Church of England now. One of the first sermons John heard at Oxford hammered home the Gospel truth from the fifth chapter of First John. "Remember this, brothers," the pastor reasoned. "That 'This is love for God: to obey his commands. And his commands are not burdensome.' "

"Who can argue with Saint John?" John responded agreeably.

But soon he realized, as his brother and father did, that this wonderful Gospel truth was being used to ignore sin. There was no more effort to address social ills than throwing loose change at the poor—if the poor happened to be standing near a tavern. Drinking night or day, seductions of innocent maidens, cheating on tests and lying seemed to be the focus of most undergraduates. Even many of their mentors, the tutors and dons, sinned. John realized he should be most grateful that both his first tutor, George Wigann, and his successor, Henry Sherman, were sober, studious men.

The debauchery slowed John's own social development. He withdrew from many of his peers. It was only after gradually acquiring friends of his own temperate habits that he began to be invited to homes in the London area and meet young ladies. Socializing soon made him realize the isolation of the rectory at Epworth had made him ignorant of his father's standing. His father Samuel was well-connected. He was a personal friend of the famous writer Daniel Defoe. Alexander Pope and Jonathan Swift critiqued his father's poetry, although not always kindly. Yes, his father was known in England.

"Most surprising," John told himself, "is the fact that my father has been in the king's court." And someone reminded John his mother's uncle was Thomas Fuller, a very well-known chaplain for King Charles the First.

John was not shy with young ladies, having grown up with seven sisters. But he had much to learn about appealing to their tender nature. He intently watched the manners of the landed gentry and listened well. Being poetic helped, too. And soon, much to his amazement, he was writing flirty letters to young ladies he had met.

"My very dearest Varanese," he would mumble as he wrote, chuckling over the code name for Sally Kirkham. His own secret name was "Cyrus." But his feelings for Sally were strong. Was she his Eve? And would she have him? He found a looking glass and took stock of himself.

"Five feet and four inches tall. One hundred and twenty pounds of lean. A firm, athletic step. Face with nothing out of proportion and calmly disposed. Shaved clean as an apple. Healthy complexion. Forehead, smooth, high and wide. Piercing eyes, set like almonds. Thin nose. Strong jaw. Dimpled chin. Lips, small but shapely. Hair, parted in middle, shiny brown, to shoulders. Eyebrows, thin but distinct. All in all, neither the ugliest nor the most handsome gentleman in England, but alert and healthy."

But when he thought about actually uniting with Sally as Adam did with Eve, John was frightened. He couldn't seem to separate her from his feelings for his sisters. It was wrong to think such thoughts. It was unthinkable.

But he flirted nevertheless. "On a high, spiritual plane," he assured himself, "where love is purest. No less than agape."

As his graduation approached, he agonized over what direction his life should take. Would he without question become a minister of the church as his father and Sammy had done? Of course not. He questioned everything. Just following the footsteps of his father and Sammy was no compelling reason to become a church cleric. On the other hand, he mustn't let their careers force him away from it, either. He must decide on the merits. But he was so close to the church.

For once, his mind was muddled. It was a shame he couldn't consult his brothers. Sammy would give him too much advice. Charles was too much a youngster. John wrote his father and mother for advice. His mother Susanna encouraged him. Much to his surprise, his father Samuel wrote:

> *As to what you mention of entering the Holy Orders, it is indeed a great work, and I am pleased to find you think so. As to the motives you take notice of, my thoughts are. . .it is no harm to desire getting into that office, even as Eli's sons, to eat a piece of bread. . .but the principal spring and motive, to which all the former should only be secondary, must certainly be the glory of God, and the service of His church in the edification of our neighbor. . . .*

That last criterion seemed to free John's thinking. Was his ambition to merely find a cozy position? Or did he really want to work for the glory of God?

He thought about it for a long time. . . .

four

The Quest for Holiness

I will indeed become a cleric of the Church of England!" he blurted one day in 1724 in his study. The truth came to John mysteriously, as it had before when he felt the presence of God. Where was the reason? Surely it was there. He just suddenly knew he would be a cleric like his father: uncompromising and exasperating. But perhaps he could be more tactful than his father. There were those who could apply the whip and still be loved. Wasn't his mother that way?

Shortly after John's decision, his father Samuel added a second rectory to his duties. Now he slogged through the marshes to Wroot, five miles from Epworth. Both rectories were more than one man could handle. John knew what his father was thinking. It wasn't just the added money. With two sons in Holy Orders, surely one would succeed him. His father expected one of the sons one day to step in and take over Wroot. Then perhaps, in time, that son would take over Epworth. That way John's mother and remaining sisters at home would not be put out on the street upon Samuel's death.

John's father was a well-worn fifty-nine. He had fallen from horses and been dragged. He had tromped up to sixteen miles some days on foot. The following spring of 1725 offered him no relief: a small stroke crippled his right hand. He was indeed in decline.

Wroot was pastoral. To some of John's sisters, the Wroot rectory and its acreage with livestock was little more than a farm that had to be tended. They were now there, off and on, all year long. Sammy visited, then teased his baby sister Kezzy with a poem:

> *The spacious glebe around the house*
> *Afford full pasture to the cows,*
> *Whence largely milky nectar flows,*
> *O sweet and cleanly dairy!*
> *Unless or Moll or Anne, or you,*
> *Your duty should neglect to do,*
> *And then 'ware haunches black and blue*
> *By pinching of a fairy.*
>
> *Observe the warmth, well littered sty,*
> *Where sows and pigs and porklets lie;*
> *Nancy or you the draff supply;*
> *They swill and care not whither.*
> *. . . but not so glad*
> *As you to wait upon your Dad!*
> *Oh, tis exceedingly pretty!*
> *Methinks I see you striving all*
> *Who first shall answer to his call,*
> *Or lusty Anne, or feeble Moll,*
>
> *Sage Pat, or sober Hetty;*
> *To rub his cassock's draggled tail,*
> *Or reach his hat from off the nail,*
> *Or seek the key to draw his ale*
> *When damsel haps to steal it.*
> *To burn his pipe, or mend his clothes,*
> *Or nicely darn his russet hose*

36

> *For comfort of his aged toes*
> *So fine they cannot feel it.*

But Hetty, the most poetic of the sisters, found no rustic comfort in Wroot. She wrote bitterly:

> *Fortune has fix'd thee in a place*
> *Debarred of wisdom, wit and grace.*
> *High births and virtue equally they scorn,*
> *As asses dull, on dunghills born;*
> *Impervious as the stones, their heads are*
> *   found;*
> *Their rage and hatred steadfast as the*
> *   ground.*
> *With these unpolished wights thy youthful*
> *   days*
> *Glide slow and dull, and nature's lamp*
> *   decays;*
> *Oh what a lamp is hid midst such a sordid*
> *   race.*

Soon the whole Wesley family was reeling from sister Hetty's departure in summer 1725. At the rectory in Epworth, father had almost locked Hetty up to keep her away from a suitor he thought a scoundrel. But she slipped out to elope with him.

Father was right. After one night of lechery, the man decided he did not want to marry Hetty after all. She returned in disgrace. Both parents were very hard on her. A marriage was arranged hastily with plumber William Wright, and she left for London.

"She is not to set foot again in the rectory," whispered wide-eyed Patty to John.

"Be patient, Patty," John counseled.

Family affairs could be so heartbreaking.

By the time John was ordained in fall 1725, he had decided to stay at Oxford—if he could get a fellowship. After all, ministers in the church had choices how to work for the glory of God. They could pastor or teach others. John stayed at Christ Church to work on his master's degree.

He had led his first successful conversion to Christianity, too: a fellow student and good friend, Robin Griffiths. Griffiths had converted John, in a sense, as well. It was he who had introduced John to Sally Kirkham and the bright social scene in the Cotswolds west of Oxford.

John's health now frightened him. One time his nose suddenly bled so severely while he was walking outside that he dived into a river nearby. As usual, he sought books for an answer. He began to study Dr. Cheyne's *Book of Health and Long Life*. He rigorously followed the advice: no salt or heavy seasoning, no pork, lots of water and vegetables. A habit of exercise was important, too. And John walked constantly.

"Now it's up to you, God," John admitted. And his health improved.

The spiritual life also had to be exercised. He preached his first sermon at the village church of Leigh on September 26, 1725. He bought a horse and stabled it nearby so he could ride to local churches to preach when opportunities came.

John began to investigate the spiritual life with more rigor than ever. He read the Medieval devotional classic *The Imitation of Christ* by Thomas à Kempis, a German monk. Its message of God's law in the heart inspired him. But it was austere, too. It rejected the material world. Surely no man but a monk could maintain such a pious life.

"I don't want to be a recluse," John said. "How does one deal with the real world?"

He read the works of William Law. Law was a forty-four-year-old cleric who had refused to swear allegiance to King George. John himself was loyal to King George. He might have felt disdain for Law had not his mother Susanna harbored similar thoughts toward the king. It was a sore point between John's parents. Samuel was fiercely loyal to the crown. Susanna considered George an impostor; the House of Hanover could not replace the House of Stuart. Because of his mother's attitude, John could read William Law without prejudice. *A Practical Treatise Upon Christian Perfection* encouraged the ideal Christian life through self-denial, humility and self-control. Law emphasized one cannot be half a Christian, but must seek moral perfection. And he stressed happiness is not found in the world but in holiness.

John liked the ideal of holiness very much. But William Law said to deny reason and trust the "witness of the Holy Spirit." Deny reason? That enlisted mysticism. John didn't like the sound of that, even though he himself had reached decisions that seemed to transcend reason.

"Why not visit William Law?" Charles suggested to John on one of their visits. "He lives at Putney, just southwest of London."

"A mass of imperfection like me? And how do you know so much about William Law?" asked John, who regarded seventeen-year-old Charles as clever but carefree. "Is it possible you're reforming?"

"Too soon for that, Brother," Charles snapped, and changed the subject.

John read the works of the seventeenth-century Anglican bishop Jeremy Taylor, especially *The Rule and Exercises of Holy Living* (1650) and *The Rule and Exercises of Holy Dying* (1651). Intended by Taylor as guides for those seekers not served by local clergy, they were already considered classics. They appealed to John very much. Taylor's counsel seemed exactly right. Piety required much self-examination. Wandering thoughts constantly had to be admonished. The world would steal a man's attention at any time. Prayers should be short and pithy, not long petitions. In the duty for God, time should not be wasted.

Taylor's advice seemed perfect for dealing with the real world. After all, hadn't Taylor done so himself? Hadn't he been a chaplain for King Charles in the Civil War? Hadn't he been imprisoned for his loyalty? And it didn't hurt his image with John that he was a graduate of Oxford.

John's quest for holiness demanded a detailed diary full of painful self-examination. So he began to record his most intimate thoughts in code. He reveled in the quest for holiness. It seemed almost too much fun. Shouldn't there be pain? Shouldn't there be sacrifice? And his quest did not prevent him from mulling over the relationship of material science with Christianity. He read books on chemistry, magnetism and gravity. Deciding true science upheld religion—because it was only a reflection of the Creator's universe—he put that question of discord aside. Others could make whatever controversy they wished over the compatibility of science and religion, but to John, the issue was closed.

John was certainly no throwback to ancient martyrs. Even the most devout clerics of England in the 1700s seemed to live life to the fullest. They did not live like aesthetes. The majority were what his father Samuel disdained as "fox-hunting parsons." They were popular with their flock and offered rituals and comfort.

It was to this life that Oxford seemed to nudge John. John himself not only learned to dance, but tried to learn every new dance. He played cards and backgammon. He indulged in chess. He mastered billiards. He played tennis. He frequented pubs. He picked berries to make his own wine. He went to horse races. He attended plays. He flirted, even touched, although he felt terrible remorse afterward.

He moved in a social circle of several prominent families in the Cotswolds. All in all, he was becoming quite the young gentleman—a gentleman who just happened to be a learned cleric.

But Sally Kirkham was not to be part of his destiny. She married a local schoolmaster less than a year after John met her. He brooded. What had happened? Had he been too vague of his intentions? Was she merely carrying on a shallow flirtation with him? Was he not her social equal? Were his prospects too dismal for a lady of her standing in society? Did he not know how to behave himself?

In such polite society one would never know the reasons. Even his good friend Robin Griffiths couldn't tell him. And yet in his heart he was relieved that Sally evaporated from his thoughts. He had thought the unthinkable about her too many times.

In June 1726, brother Charles arrived at Christ Church College in Oxford, almost the very day John was leaving. "Have fun running the farm at Wroot this summer," Charles joked.

"Behave yourself here, Charles," John said. He was not joking.

That summer John was curate for his father's rectory at Wroot. He delivered some hard sermons, and they were not well-received. He was learning what his father had endured for so many years. The flock did not appreciate correction. Nor did his father and mother. Hetty had been trying to reconcile with them by letter, getting only sharp responses in return.

For the first time, John began to appreciate his sisters'

41

dilemma. They thought themselves far too educated and refined to enjoy the company of illiterate farmers and small tradesmen. Yet they were so poorly clothed they could not mingle with their social and intellectual peers. They were looked down upon. It was tragic.

Its most visible victim was Hetty, treated like a common tart by one of the gentry. To compound the pain, now Hetty was treated the same way by her parents. So John gave a sermon on unconditional love, so pointedly aimed at his parents that both were angered. Father Samuel was so indignant he actually considered asking the bishop to reprimand John.

"What high church self-righteousness!" John later said to Patty.

"Will we ever see such behavior in yourself?" she replied slyly.

Outside the pulpit, John rode and picked berries and swam and hunted plover—when he was not flirting with young ladies like Kitty Hargreaves. He justified his flirtations by reading serious literature like Spenser's *Fairie Queen* with her. He had long, searching discussions with his mother, who was a rigid disciplinarian but more flexible than his father. It was a good life. Too bad his own father never learned how to relax a bit, get some balance between work and leisure and enjoy the fruits of life.

"John," cautioned his mother Susanna, "aren't you living the life of a squire?"

"I've read all about the self-sacrifices one can make in *The Imitation of Christ*," he explained calmly. With utter conviction, he added, "I don't think that when God sent us into the world He had irreversibly decreed that we should be perpetually miserable in it. Why does the psalmist exhort us to rejoice in the Lord and tell us that it becomes the just to be joyful?"

Life at Wroot went on in this stylish mode for John. He was disappointed when Kitty was sent away abruptly by her parents, and wondered if his father had been meddling. John was seen by many now as a man who knew how to get along. Yes, he was a cleric, but a wise and worldly one—not a self-righteous nuisance like his father. His father should have been a bishop by now, many said.

Then John received wonderful news. He had been elected a fellow at Lincoln College at Oxford, a post so prestigious his father bubbled with delight. This was a boon of lifetime proportions, for it was truly for life—so long as the fellow didn't marry.

"The fellow even has living quarters in the college for life!" his father enthused.

Never to marry? John considered the finality of that. In his heart, he felt relieved. For whatever reasons, physical intimacy frightened him. Had Saint Paul the same feelings?

John ultimately convinced himself this appointment at Lincoln College must the hand of God. How then could he refuse? He accepted. The college graciously allowed him to remain for the time being at Wroot, helping his father.

John's fervor for righteousness in the pulpit ebbed and flowed. But every time he preached the hard life of righteousness to his flock, they seethed in their pews. "Why didn't he just stick to the liturgy and give a sermon on love?" they grumbled.

"No wonder my father's life has been such a battle," John told himself, remembering the maimed livestock and burning rectory. John was as ambivalent about his father now as his sisters and Charles were. He was irritated by his father's stiff-necked intolerance and meddling, yet loved his courage and dogged persistence. Only Sammy did not seem to see the exasperating, meddlesome side of his father.

In January 1727, just days after John had talked to Robin Griffiths, he learned Robin had died. "Praise God," John thought in his sorrow, "that I offered Robin salvation and he took it."

John now felt the poignant power of the earnest cleric. It was so much more noble than scrambling after and pawing objects of the flesh. Certainly his life was headed in the right direction.

At home with John's parents now were only Kezzy, seventeen; Patty, twenty; and Molly, thirty-one. Patty was to leave soon to live with Uncle Matthew in London. Emily, thirty-six, lived and worked in boarding schools with the thought of opening her own. Sukey had married farmer Richard Ellison, a man considered very coarse by the Wesleys. "He's a constant affliction to the family," whispered Susanna. Robust Anne had married John Lambert, a land surveyor. Anne had given birth to a son the previous summer. John, the godfather, had danced at the party following the christening.

"Watch out for poor Richard," some whispered. "He is much too fond of his liquor." And John heard his sisters whispering of these flaws. Hetty's husband William Wright was not spared; he, too, was said to be a drinker.

In 1728, John was ordained a priest in the Church of England. But his extended stay at Wroot had undermined his decision to be the Oxford scholar. Still unmarried, still trying to suppress lusty thoughts, he found himself vacillating among three choices: the life of a hard-hitting preacher, the life of a "fox-hunting parson" or the life of an Oxford cleric.

Finally, his colleagues at Oxford helped him choose. By late 1729, they had tired of the constant leaves of absence of their fellow. If John wanted to keep his post at Lincoln College, he had better return and help out full-time.

"It seems I'm to be an Oxford fellow—or else," he told his

father. "And, of course, a fellow can't marry," he added unnecessarily.

By November 1729, John was back at Lincoln College. His specialties were classics, divinity and logic. He reinstituted the rigorous schedule he had set up in 1727 and then had aban-doned for Wroot. Sunday was the day he devoted to divinity. Monday and Tuesday were Greek and Latin. Wednesday was logic and ethics. Thursday was Hebrew and Arabic. Friday was metaphysics and natural philosophy. Saturday was oratory and poetry. He also tutored and judged debates several times a week!

Lincoln College had been founded in 1427 by Robert Fleming for the express purpose of defending the faith against uneducated louts who might dare to preach the Gospel. This very conservative goal did not disturb John at all. It was clear enough to him that the uneducated should not preach the Gospel. After all, he had had to read volumes and volumes to reach his own understanding of the Gospel.

It was nice that John could amble across High Street and check on brother Charles at Christ Church once in a while. "Oh, and I mustn't forget brother Charles's little club of three or four students," he remembered.

According to Charles, in a moment of inspiration several months earlier he had started a club of like minds to try to live up to the ideals espoused by the statutes of Oxford. As students, they were supposed to discipline their lives. They resolved to study the curriculum hard, pray hard, study the Bible and rigorously attend Holy Communion, just as the statutes demanded.

"No one is less rigorous than my brother Charles," John told his friends in wonder. "Can he be serious?"

Charles was poetic, undisciplined. He suffered from a lack of money far more than John. For three years as an

45

undergraduate at Christ Church, he had been enchanted with everything Epworth never had. He adored plays. He was infatuated with actresses. And he had magnetism. How else could he have become captain of his class at Westminster?

But pious? Never. Once, when John had reprimanded Charles for his playful habits, his brother had quipped, "What, would you have me be a saint all at once?"

Yet upon learning John was returning to Oxford, Charles had written him:

> *I hope that I shall [not] relapse into my former state of insensibility. It is through your means, I firmly believe, that God will establish what He has begun in me; and there is no person I shall so willingly have to be the instrument of good to me as you. It is owing, in great measure, to somebody's prayers (my mother's most likely) that I am come to think as I do; for I cannot tell myself how or when I awoke from my lethargy—only that it was not long after you went away.*

Could this prodigal brother be serious? More amazing yet, could he be the founder of a group devoted to piety and discipline?

John began to suspect Charles might be sincere when he heard the tiny club ridiculed and scorned as the "Holy Club" by other undergraduates. When he first sat in on the club, he knew Charles really had changed. Charles was dead serious about living a hard, pious life.

Naturally, John took over the club. Hadn't the letter from Charles suggested that? He expanded its goals. In addition to the goals Charles already had set, they began rigorously to read and discuss the classics three or four nights a week. They reviewed a religious work on Sunday.

During those early days, there were just two other members besides John and Charles. Francis Gore had been a friend of Charles since Westminster. William Morgan was an intense Irish youth. Soon they were joined by John's old friend Robert Kirkham of the Cotswold scene. Members drifted in and out. Membership was usually never more than a dozen.

Word of their club reached the rest of the Wesley family. Brother Sammy did not like such splinter groups. But Samuel was ecstatic. He wrote John:

> *I hear my son has the honor of being styled the Father of the Holy Club, and if it be so, I must be the Grandfather of it. . . . I have the highest reason to bless God that He has given me two sons together at Oxford to whom He has given grace and courage to turn the war against the world and the devil.*

During summer 1730, the club passed beyond the quiet rigor of meetings in the womb of Oxford into the prisons and slums of the real world. . . .

five

The Methodist

*I*t was fiery William Morgan who first started to venture out from Oxford. "I've visited a convicted murderer in prison," he told the others.

The others followed his example. But before plunging too deeply into prison ministry, John talked to the local bishop and the prison warden. With their blessings, the Holy Club forged ahead. The club visited prisons and helped raise money to support the poor families of the prisoners outside of prison.

Helping poor families educated John about the pitiful amount of money common people earned. Laborers and sailors were lucky to earn twenty pounds in a year. John's own family had struggled on well more than a hundred pounds a year.

William seemed bursting with good ideas. He next started a school for the children of the prisoners. Father Samuel Wesley enthused, "I think I must adopt Mr. Morgan to be my son."

The Holy Club members began to raise money to get debtors out of prison. Whatever their club was going to be, it was not going to be a monastic society. They were definitely not withdrawing from the world.

And how slackers hate the righteous. Undergraduates called them "Bible Bigots" and much worse. A few of the kinder students referred to them as "methodists." And the best taunts in these poetic days were always in rhyme:

> *By rule they eat, by rule they drink,*
> *Do all things else by rule, but think—*
> *Accuse their priests of loose behavior,*
> *To get more in the laymen's favor;*
> *Method alone must guide 'em all,*
> *Whence Methodists themselves they call.*

If a gulf developed between these few pious men and the undergraduates, John discovered there was also a great gulf between himself and the common people they were helping. When he spoke to the poor inside and outside prison, he realized they gaped at him in wonder. Was it his vestments? Surely they had seen ministers before. His face? Surely his face radiated only sincerity. His smell? He was as clean as any other in these times.

"Pray, sir," he privately asked one of the more articulate prisoners, "for what reason do the prisoners gawk at me so boldly?"

"Ain't nothing but blooming bewilderment, sir."

"You mean they have no idea what I'm saying!" John blurted in amazement.

"They catch a word every once in a while, sir."

John had to think about that. This language barrier had enormous implications. Did the common people not understand any of the rich language of the liturgy? What was a minister to do? The liturgy could not even be changed by one word, let alone be abandoned. That was certain.

John realized the commoners must be educated. In the meantime, he would try to find simple words to express himself in his sermons, just so long as they meant what he thought in more explicit words. But was that possible? All he could do was try. So he made an effort to use common, easy words, but pure and proper.

He could spew his pent-up poetry on paper, for once again John was corresponding with a lady of the Cotswolds. It seemed perfectly harmless, even holy. Mrs. Pendarves of Buckland, the former Mary Granville, was a young widow three years older than John. At thirty she was a much-desired lady, her beauty and wit praised even in London, where she was known in the king's court. The famous composer Handel, kept by the court, was devoted to her. He had written her faithfully since she was nineteen. It was flattering to John to correspond with such a coveted lady.

And he was challenged, too. Could he hold his own in such clever company? Month after month the two exchanged witty letters when not actually seeing each other occasionally at parties and weddings. From the beginning, John candidly admitted he was leery of risking his heart again, after being wounded by Sally Kirkham. This was his way of warning Mary Pendarves she mustn't expect anything more than a platonic, spiritual friend in John. Love, yes—but it was agape, the purest love of total commitment.

"But John," Charles advised, "she will think that is your way of telling her how much you adore her."

"Nonsense. You don't know the lady. She is not interested in lustful attentions. She has the same kind of purely friendly attention from Handel himself."

So John encouraged and flattered her and she encouraged and flattered him. In spite of himself, he once again showered the "love" of his life with words of affection but no solid intentions.

And was he a righteous enough confidant for the much admired Mrs. Pendarves? By July 1731 he could not keep from extolling the righteousness he had gained from his association with the Holy Club, and complain of his detractors. He read that portion of his letter to Charles:

51

*I have been charged with being too strict,
with carrying things too far in religion, and
laying burdens on myself, if not others, which
were neither necessary nor possible to be
borne. A heavy charge indeed! To be too
strict! That is to blaspheme the law of God as
not strict enough. To carry duties too far!
Why, what is this but to change holiness itself
into extravagance?*

Charles paled. "Are you sure you want to say quite that much to Mrs. Pendarves?"

"Isn't it true? Besides, it's not the strongest portion of my letter. Listen to this." And John read:

*Do not blame me. . .for appealing to the
judgment of one who in this is not likely to
be prejudiced in my favor. Those among
whom chiefly your lot is cast are not accused
of too much strictness. Whatever ill weeds
may flourish there, a Court is not fit soil for
this. . . .*

Charles's jaw dropped. "Surely you won't mail that."

"Certainly. If she is a saintly woman, it will ring true."

"The acorn doesn't fall far from the tree, Brother," Charles muttered. "That personal touch is worthy of our father in its honesty and crushing lack of tact."

John was miffed. Everyone knew Charles was the son most like their father. "But is the letter true, Brother?"

"Yes," Charles grumbled. "Oh, well, perhaps this is best," he added softly.

In her next letter, Mary Pendarves icily told John he was

"really in a state to be envied." She asked John to please destroy her previous letters. After that frosty communication, she no longer answered his letters. So John realized he had irritated her with his bragging of personal righteousness. And he had to admit that in some ways young Charles, in spite of his impulsiveness and hot temper, was his superior in tact and social graces. Yes, he had to think of Charles now as almost his equal.

John received sickening news from Epworth in summer 1731. Mother Susanna wrote that she, Father Samuel, Patty and two servants had been riding in their open wagon. She and Samuel sat in chairs. Suddenly the horses bolted. Susanna described the scene:

> . . . .*Out flew your father and his chair. . . [after which] two neighbors. . .raised his head, upon which he had pitched, and held him backwards, by which means he began to [breathe again]; for it is certain, by the blackness of his face, that he had never drawn breath from the time of his fall till they helped him up. . . .He looked prodigiously wild, but. . .said he knew nothing of any fall, he was as well as ever he was in his whole life. . . .*

Susanna went on to detail how badly injured Samuel's head was, and the following days of stiffness and pain and illness. Samuel returned to the pulpit, but much diminished. He betrayed his own doubts by imploring his sons, especially Sammy, to succeed him at Epworth. John had thought of that inevitable day often. Now his father's demise was more apparent than ever.

William Morgan, such an innovator for the Holy Club, became very ill in summer 1732. William had often fasted severely. Had it ruined his health? Sometimes it seemed to John that William was actually dying before his eyes. Or was William leveled by the displeasure of his father in Ireland? Even in Ireland, his father had heard terrible stories about their club of lunatics entering poor people's homes, teaching their children prayers, giving them money, and so on. He threatened to send William no more money. Finally, he demanded that William return to Dublin.

"We owe so much to William Morgan," John lamented. "I can hardly bear his leaving. Let us pray he will soon return."

That same summer, John met a man who had greatly influenced his ideas about holiness, William Law. Law recently had written his best work yet: *A Serious Call to a Devout and Holy Life*. John journeyed to Law's home in Putney, southwest of London. Because Law disavowed King George and his successor George the Second, he was not allowed to perform his Holy Orders. He made his living by tutoring students. In his garden, Law urged John to read *Theologica Germanica* and other mystical writings.

"Everything seems to reinforce our decision to seek the holy life," John told Charles.

About this same time, John became a member of the Society for Promoting Christian Knowledge in London. He was attracted to the society because it encouraged evangelizing in prisons, but he soon learned it had a two-pronged attack. In foreign lands, the society not only evangelized but established colonies for debtors from English prisons.

In the society, John met James Oglethorpe, who was leaving on a great venture. He was going to found such a colony for debtors in America. The colony would be named Georgia after King George.

With Kezzy, John two years before had gone to see "Indian kings" brought from America to London by Sir Coming. These "kings," called Cherokees, were stolid. They changed John's mind about heathens. They were not gibbering simians but reserved, even noble, humans. Intelligence radiated from their dark eyes.

What would it be like to go to Oglethorpe's Georgia and bring these very attractive people to Christ?

Then in August 1732, John's world crashed. "William Morgan dead?" he cried.

"Yes," Charles said. "He simply died in Ireland. His father blames us."

John was even more distressed when he read the father's letter. Days later, he sent a very tactful response to William's father. He explained in detail how the club had originated and what it had accomplished. His explanation was so effective that in the following months the father actually entrusted the care of his youngest son Richard to John at Oxford.

One September morning in 1733, Charles visited John at Lincoln College. John was mildly surprised. "So early, Charles? We're not meeting until tonight."

"One of the poor apple women at our college came to me. There is a woman in the workhouse who tried to kill herself. She thought we might help the poor woman overcome this dread compulsion."

"Of course. We must go at once."

John learned later that an undergraduate at Pembroke College had urged the apple woman to enlist the Wesley brothers. John invited the Pembroke student to the King's Head. The young man looked uncomfortable being served. He commented that it was he who served others, as his only source of income was waiting tables himself. The poor fellow had a bright, open face but squinted grotesquely, as if his eyes were damaged. John had rarely seen a student at Oxford in such seedy clothes.

"The poor woman at the workhouse has had a change of heart," John commented, "no thanks to me or even you, but to the Lord."

"I knew you. . .I mean the Lord could save her," the student said.

"Where are you from, sir?" John asked.

"Gloucester. My mother owns the Bell Inn there. It seems like I've spent my entire life in that inn, sanding the floor and drawing ale. I must confess, Mr. Wesley, I've been watching the Methodists for a year now. I first saw you as your club was being jeered while going to Holy Communion at St. Mary's. I've wondered every day since then if I would have the courage to do that."

"Come to our club then, Mr. Whitefield, and find out."

"With your encouragement I will, sir. Gladly." George Whitefield's face glowed. That was the invitation he wanted to hear.

As busy as John was, he thought about Whitefield later. He gradually had learned from others that this student was almost a recluse, never socializing because he had no money. He studied and worked and apparently admired the Holy Club from afar. But it was Whitefield's voice that tugged at John's memory. It was very powerful, like an actor's. His pronunciation was so crisp and dramatic his words clung in John's mind.

Whitefield was a mere nineteen years old. John was now thirty, Charles almost twenty-six. John felt odd being so much older than the people he cared most to associate with. For it was not the smug faculty he cultivated, but students not yet poisoned or deadened by the world.

In January 1734, John's sister Molly married John

Whitelamb. Whitelamb was a protégé of John's father, who made him curate at the rectory in Wroot. Whitelamb had been at John's Lincoln College in Oxford for a short while.

Tragically, Molly died in childbirth within a year. Of all the sisters, Molly was the sweetest and meekest. She was buried with the baby in her arms. Whitelamb was so disconsolate that Samuel contacted James Oglethorpe and urged him to recruit Whitelamb as a pastor for Georgia. But Whitelamb remained at Wroot.

Hetty was crushed by Molly's death, too. Through all her troubles, sweet Molly had been the most sympathetic to her. Hetty wrote:

> *If highest worth, in beauty's bloom,*
> *Exempted mortals from the tomb,*
> *We had not round this sacred bier*
> *Mourned the sweetest babe and mother*
> > *here,*
> *Where innocence from harm is blest,*
> *And meek sufferer is at rest!*
> *Fierce pangs she bore without complaint,*
> *Till heaven relieved the finished saint.*
> *If savage bosoms felt her woe,*
> *Who lived and died without a foe,*
> *How should I mourn, or how commend,*
> *My tenderest, dearest, firmest friend?*
> *Most pious, meek, resigned, chaste,*
> *With every social virtue graced!*
> *If, reader, thou wouldst prove and know*
> *The ease she found not here below;*
> *Her bright example points the way,*
> *To perfect bliss and endless day.*

The Fens country seemed to intrude more and more in John's busy Oxford life now. Since May 1734, a former student at Lincoln College, Westley Hall, had been courting his youngest sister Kezzy at Epworth. Then Hall began courting John's sister Patty, who lived in London with Uncle Matthew. This strange courtship would surely cause problems within the family. John, who had introduced Westley Hall to his family, had to confront him.

"I've heard, Mister Hall, you're seeing my sister Patty."

"Pray, how could I resist? She's your twin."

"I don't see the relevance," John sniffed.

Hall was not the first to make that observation, though. Many had said that. It didn't bother John. She was certainly not his twin. She was smaller than John's five feet four inches and 120 pounds. Her thin, straight nose was not slightly bent on the end, as John's was. The dimple in her chin was not quite so pronounced as John's.

Perhaps it was the eyes more than anything. They were almond-shaped, as many Scandinavian eyes are, and some said very lively. And John had to admit she, too, had a high, wide forehead. . . .

Hall broke into his thoughts. "I only meant that was what first struck me about her. But, sir, have you not ever vacillated a time or two with the ladies? How could any gentleman choose quickly between two such choice ladies as your sisters? It's wrenching. Pray God will let me be fortunate enough to have one or the other."

Hall had the truth on his side. John, too, had deliberated over the ladies, sometimes in ecstasy, usually in guilt-ridden torment, but always long and hard. What was he to say to Hall? Was the choice of Hall's wife his? Or Hall's?

Epworth intruded more and more. John's father implored him to take the rectory. The appeal was heart-rending. His father said his work must go on—not to mention the threat of Susanna being cut adrift from the rectory.

But John simply could not go back to the confines of Epworth. Besides, he knew brother Sammy had turned down the appeal first. He wrote his father a very detailed letter mentioning the enormous satisfaction he got at Oxford with half a dozen men of his own pious leanings. That camaraderie was not to be had at Epworth. He went further:

> *I have not only as much, but as little, company as I please. I have no such thing as a trifling [visitor]. . . .No one ever takes it into his head to set foot within my door, except he has some business of importance. . .and even then, as soon as he has dispatched his business, he immediately [leaves]. . . .*

He went on to explain more conveniences:

> *Freedom from care I take to be the next greatest advantage. . . .My income is ready for me on so many stated day . . .to count and carry it home. [My greatest] expense is food, and this too is provided without any care of mine. . . .My laundress, barber, etc., are always ready. . . .*

Defensively, he insisted he was not a drone. The fact that some fellows abused the soft college life did not discredit its usefulness. As a clincher, John mentioned the vicious treatment of his father by his parishioners: throwing him in jail for debt, mysterious fires, the maimed livestock, the whispers, the stubborn refusal to repent. Should a Wesley son feel indebted to such parishioners? "In all," John boldly told Charles, "I listed twenty-six reasons why I must stay at Oxford!"

Yet John felt guilty ignoring his father's pleas. Eventually, the appeal was too much for him. John decided he must become rector of Epworth. After all, it involved the fate of mother Susanna and his sisters, too.

But then he learned his father had finally, reluctantly recommended John Romley for Epworth. Romley, the schoolmaster, had been serving as curate. John could not interfere now. The Wesleys already had hurt John Romley enough. He had courted Hetty years before—until Samuel deemed him unfit. How Romley must have ached underneath, thinking of Hetty's eventual disgrace.

"No, we must not hurt Romley again," John decided.

The year 1735 brought Samuel's health crashing down. His condition was so obviously terminal Susanna advised the children to gather. John, Charles, Emily and Kezzy were soon at their father's bedside in Epworth. The other sisters and Sammy weren't there yet. Samuel was cheerful enough. To die was gain. One of his few regrets was that his rectories would not pass on to one of his sons. Another regret was that he hadn't seen his magnum opus, the exhaustive study of Job, in print. The sons assured him they personally would see it through.

As the end neared, Samuel told John, "The inward witness, son, the inward witness, is the strongest proof of Christianity."

John was surprised. Did his father suspect John had doubts?

Samuel laid his hands on Charles's head. "Be steady. The Christian faith will surely revive in this kingdom; you shall see it, though I shall not."

Samuel Wesley died April 25, 1735. He was buried in Saint Andrew's churchyard in Epworth, joining six of his babies.

Kezzy went to Tiverton to live with Sammy. Mother Susanna went to Gainsborough to live with Emily. Both John and Charles went not to Oxford, but to London near Westminster, guests of the family of James Hutton, an Oxford friend. James ran a book shop called "Bible and Sun." There John would make sure his father's lifelong work on Job was printed.

While in Westminster, he was contacted by John Burton on behalf of none other than James Oglethorpe. "You, John Wesley, are Oglethorpe's first choice to be the chaplain of Savannah in his Georgia colony," Burton said.

"Surely this really means he intends me to pastor the Indians in Georgia," John confided to Charles later. "Pure, unspoiled. Bringing such noble peoples to Christ is very important. I'll have to deliberate much on Oglethorpe's offer."

John did think on it. In spite of his pursuit of holiness, he was very troubled. He brooded over the soft life he had chosen. And his temptations with women distressed him. Every relationship seemed plagued by his battle over deciphering his real feelings: was the lady an object of love or lust? of God or the devil?

And the death of William Morgan haunted him. Could John have prevented it? The unceasing criticism of the Holy Club at Oxford by his colleagues as well as undergraduates troubled him, too. And the club itself had never grown to more than twenty enthusiasts at one time.

Moreover, John still did not have the faith he thought some people had. The "inward witness" was missing, just as his father had suspected. Would John find real faith across the ocean in Georgia? For many years he had thought holiness could only be found when he could depend on the refuge of relative quiet and solitude at Oxford—never in the unguarded, unending busy life of a pastor. Maybe he was wrong.

He set his thoughts on paper. He pretended he was writing to Burton pleading his case, explaining his motives:

> *My chief motive to which all the rest are subordinate is the hope of saving my own soul. I hope to learn the true sense of the Gospel of Christ, by preaching it to the heathen. They have no comments to construe away the text, no vain philosophy to corrupt it, no luxurious, sensual, covetous, ambitious expounders to soften its unpleasing truths. . . .A right faith will, I trust, by the mercy of God, open the way for a right practice, especially when most of those temptations are removed which here so easily beset me. Toward mortifying the desire of the flesh, the desire of sensual pleasure, it will be no small thing to be able, without fear of giving offense, to live on water and the fruits of the earth. This simplicity of food will, I trust, be a blessed means, both in preventing my seeking that happiness in meats and drinks which God designs should be found only in faith and love and joy in the Holy Ghost, and assist me—especially where I see no woman but those which are almost a different species from me—to attain such a purity of thought as suits a candidate for that state wherein they never marry nor are given in marriage, but are as the angels of God in heaven. . . .*

He reviewed what he had written. Never had he put down his fight against desires of the flesh so plainly. But he went on to write more on other motives. He surely didn't want to sound as if his whole thinking was on the flesh.

After he had finished, he was very pleased. Never had real holiness for John seemed so attainable as in Georgia. The exercise had been most valuable.

And the thought struck him. "If I truly believe this, and my chief aim in life is to save my own soul, why not mail the letter to Burton?"

six

A Crushing Revelation

John mailed the letter to John Burton. There was much to do before sailing to America in October. First and foremost, John recruited. Before long he had two of the Holy Club members going to Georgia, too. Benjamin Ingham was a delicate man of twenty-three, all youth and impulse, determined to do good. Delamotte, twenty-one, begged to come, offering to come as John's servant, if need be.

One other remained to be recruited. John confronted him: "I believe you should accompany me." His recruit was none other than his brother Charles.

"To America!" Charles squawked undiplomatically.

"Yes, Brother."

Charles resisted. "I'm not even ordained yet."

John went to work on that. Charles also objected that he had no position in Georgia. John went to work on that, too. Within weeks, James Oglethorpe had offered Charles a position as his personal secretary. Moreover, the bishop of Oxford had agreed to ordain Charles deacon. And most shocking of all, the bishop of London agreed to ordain Charles a priest just one week later!

"I'm stunned," Charles said.

In August, John married his sister Emily to Robert Harper, a pharmacist in Epworth. Meanwhile, Westley Hall had stopped relentlessly courting back and forth between

John's sisters Patty and Kezzy. He now courted just Patty.

John began to feel Kezzy might have been wronged. He confronted Hall. "Didn't you make promises of matrimony to Kezzy first?"

Hall said, "Sir, I soured on Kezzy because of what John Whitelamb has written me about her."

Hall showed John the letter. John knew Whitelamb held a grudge against Kezzy because she had loudly opposed his marriage to Molly. Oh, family problems were so hard to resolve. Why was marriage sour for the Wesley sisters? John explained to Hall that the accusations against Kezzy were false. He even made excuses for Whitelamb's vengeful behavior.

"By building up Kezzy to Hall, did I solve anything?" John asked Charles later. "Or did I make things worse?"

Worse, John soon learned. Hall had visited Kezzy and courted her again. He even gave her a ring and promised her he would return. Two weeks later, on September 15, he married Patty in London!

"What a scoundrel!" John fumed. "What villainy can he do next?"

John soon learned of Hall's latest impudence. He was going with him to Georgia!

"No! This can't be!" John yelped. "The colony is lost."

"But it's true," Charles said, taking some small pleasure in seeing someone outmaneuver his domineering brother. "He's getting quick ordinations from the bishop of London—just like you got for me. And he's got an official appointment for Georgia—just like you got for me."

"He's the most blatant opportunist known to mankind." John felt sick. "And this wretch is going to be in Georgia with us? Causing God only knows what kind of trouble for us?"

"Pray, Brother, pray."

John did pray. And when the gentlemen from Oxford sailed down the Thames from Westminster to Gravesend in early October 1735, remaining behind in London was Westley Hall. He had decided to pursue interests there for a while. Had Uncle Matthew sweetened the pot for Hall in London? *Praise the Lord,* John thought. But he knew in his heart that problems with Hall were not over. He prayed for Patty and Uncle Matthew.

One of John's last duties before embarking was most pleasant. He had the enviable task of delivering his father's book on Job to Queen Caroline herself. She had granted him an audience. Caroline pretended sometimes to be flighty and frivolous, but she was no empty-headed coquette; she was middle-aged, shrewd and very influential with the king. Sometimes she truly ran the government when the king was off tending to his affairs in Germany. John was nervous as he was called into a royal chamber to present Her Highness with the bound volume.

"It is very prettily bound," she said graciously. Then she laid it down.

"Thank you, Your Highness," John replied. He bowed and withdrew.

At Gravesend, the four Oxford men boarded the *Simmonds,* one of two large passenger vessels sailing together. James Oglethorpe would be aboard the *Simmonds* and generously had reserved two cabins for the Oxford men in the fore-castle. The Wesleys had the larger one, Delamotte and Ingham the other. There were other cabins. Oglethorpe had the largest. Directly above the Wesleys were the William Hortons. Three other cabins were for the surgeon Dr. Thomas Hawkins and his wife Beata, for carpenter John Welch and his wife Ann, and for the Richard Lawleys. Both Ann Welch and Mrs. Lawley were pregnant. Most passengers had no cabins but slept below deck. In all, more than a hundred passengers were sailing for America.

"Not a moment to waste, gentlemen," John said to his companions.

So as they waited for a favorable wind, the four Oxford men, true to form, set up a rigorous schedule. John just recently had experimented with his own sleep. For years he had awaked to an alarm at eight o'clock. He began gradually cutting back the waking hour until it felt just right. Now he woke at four o'clock, felt no fatigue all day and went to sleep immediately upon retiring. So now all four men rose at four and prayed privately for one hour before meeting to read the Bible from five to seven.

From eight to nine were public prayers. About forty passengers attended. Not attending because they held their own service were twenty-six Moravians, led by their bishop David Nitschmann. They all followed a German religious reformer, Count Zinzendorf. He had pulled away from the Lutheran Church in 1727. These Moravians practiced a mystical form of Christianity and claimed to be exceedingly pious. It was not long before John realized the Moravians were trying to live the holiness advocated by William Law, who was also a mystic.

John whispered to Charles, "Let us watch these Moravians closely. Just how effective is this mystical form of Christianity?"

From nine to twelve, the four Oxford men did their own private business. John could not miss the opportunity to learn German from the Moravians. Delamotte usually studied Greek. Charles wrote sermons or hymns. Ingham usually instructed children. At noon, the four met to discuss their day and plans for tomorrow. This web of checks and cross-checks prevented backsliding. They had a pact: none did anything without the knowledge of the others.

After lunch, they spoke and read the Gospel to people until four. Four to five was public prayer, five to six private prayer, six to seven evangelizing English passengers in their cabin, and seven to eight joining the Moravians for their evening service. At eight the four met again to exhort each other. Their pact was so strong that every individual undertaking had to be approved by the others. They had a rigid method for voting on this, and if there was a two-to-two disagreement, the matter was decided by lot.

Between nine and ten they fell asleep.

John did not neglect his duty to see that sin did not engulf the ship. He complained to Oglethorpe about many sins. Oglethorpe accommodated him. A boy was whipped for swearing and blaspheming. The Hortons' maid was ordered ashore for being drunk and immoral. John's righteousness was not universally admired; many passengers resented him. Not the least was Horton, who for several nights stomped the floor above the Wesleys' cabin to keep him awake.

"Did you not consider the Hortons were directly above us, John?" Charles asked groggily.

John's own life became even more regimented. He continued to keep a diary in code of everything he did every hour of the day; now, at night, he summarized his day in a journal. Sometimes his journal entry was very long and sometimes very short, but it was always relevant. For November 23, after being at sea a few weeks in the escort now of the *Hawk,* a British man-of-war ship, he entered:

> *At night I awaked by the tossing of the ship*
> *and roaring of the wind, and plainly showed*
> *I was unfit, for I was unwilling to die.*

To John, a willingness to die was an ultimate test of faith. He remembered well how William Morgan had had no fear of dying. His father Samuel had had no fear of dying. But John feared it. And that fear haunted him. It was further proof he was still only half a Christian. At times he wondered if he was fit to instruct others. He knew no one he could ask for advice.

Still, he persisted. Beata Hawkins in particular challenged him. She was a very attractive, bubbly woman, but could John deny her the Gospel because she was too becoming? She said her mother was very pious but died when Beata was ten, so she herself had little religious training. She was willing, so John spent much time with her. When she batted her doe-like eyes, she seemed a very conscience-stricken lady.

In January 1736, the *Simmonds* neared America. Fair weather was a paradox. It seemed to afford the time for much squabbling aboard. Passengers first had become impatient, then quarrelsome. Many claimed lasting enmities. John acted peacemaker, but not very successfully.

But on January 17, the squabbling yielded to a greater battle. John wrote in his journal:

> *At seven in the evening they were quieted by a storm. It rose higher and higher till nine. About nine the sea broke over us from stem to stern; burst through the windows of the state cabin, where three or four of us were, and covered us all over, though a bureau sheltered me from the main shock. About eleven I lay down in the great cabin, and in a short while fell asleep, although very uncertain whether I should wake alive, and much ashamed of my unwillingness to die.*

A week later, a second storm battered the ship. At one point John stepped out of his cabin and the sea swept across the deck in full tide, completely uprooting and enveloping him. He thought for horrifying moments he would surface far out at sea, away from the ship. But somehow he remained on deck, unharmed.

Two days later, they encountered a third storm. This time John wrote in his journal:

> *. . . I went to the Germans. I had long before observed the great seriousness of their behavior. Of their humility they had given a continual proof, by performing those servile offices for other passengers, which none of the English would undertake; for which they desired, and would receive no pay, saying, "it was good for their proud hearts," and "their loving Savior had done more for them." And every day had given them an occasion of showing a meekness, which no injury could move. If they were pushed, struck, or thrown down, they rose again and went away; but no complaint was found in their mouth. There was now an opportunity of trying whether they were delivered from the spirit of fear, as well as from that of pride, anger and revenge.*
>
> *In the midst of the psalm wherewith their service began, the sea broke over, split the mainsail in pieces, covered the ship, and poured in between the decks, as if the great deep had already swallowed us up. A terrible*

> *screaming began among the English. The Germans calmly sung on. I asked one of them afterwards, "[Were] you not afraid?" He answered, "I thank God, no." I asked, "But were not your women and children afraid?" He replied mildly, "No; our women and children are not afraid to die."*

There it was again: faith so strong that death held no terror. The English passengers did not have it. And worse of all, John did not have it. All his rigor, all his desire for holiness, all his reason could not give it to him. And yet all the Moravians had it!

On February 4 at noon, sailors on the mast saw darkness on the horizon. It was not another storm. It was the forests of America. The trees loomed larger. A few hours later, those on the main deck saw the trees. One day later, the *Simmonds* and the other passenger vessel anchored in the mouth of the Savannah River near Tybee Island. Oglethorpe took a boat upriver to his settlement at Savannah. He said he would return the next day with the Moravian leader August Spangenberg.

John went ashore to an uninhabited island and later enthused over America in his journal:

> *The pines, palms and cedars running in rows along the shore made an exceedingly beautiful prospect, especially to us who did not expect to see the bloom of spring in the depth of winter. The clearness of the sky, the setting sun, the smoothness of the water conspired to recommend this new world and prevent our regretting the loss of our native country.*

John returned to the *Simmonds* to discover their idyllic wait for Oglethorpe's return was marred by peddlers coming to the vessel to sell a cask of rum. Many passengers were already drunk. John, never hesitant to act against sin, smashed the rum barrel, in spite of threats and curses. "Father would have been proud of you," Charles said nervously.

When Oglethorpe returned, he brought fresh beef, pork, venison, turkeys, bread and turnips. The people's anger over John's destruction of the rum dissolved under their desire to feast. Fresh food at last!

Food was not on John's mind. He sought out the Moravian leader Spangenberg, who had returned with Oglethorpe. His cowardice aboard ship haunted him.

"Herr Spangenberg, how is it the youngest Moravian has no fear of death, and I am fearful?"

"My brother, I must first ask you one or two questions. Have you the witness within yourself? Does the Spirit of God bear witness with your spirit, that you are a child of God?"

John could not fathom what Spangenberg meant. It sounded like the same thing his father had said. It seemed William Law had said something similar. John was speechless.

Spangenberg continued, "Do you know Jesus Christ?"

"I know He is the Savior of the world."

"True, but do you know He has saved you?"

"I do," John answered, but now he knew in his heart he did not know that. He believed it only with his head. Deep inside, he did not believe Jesus had died specifically for him, John Wesley. What a crushing revelation!

Herr Spangenberg seemed a man truly in Christ.

Something else bothered John: his commitment to save Beata Hawkins had resulted in them spending many hours together. And he couldn't seem to stay away from her. John asked, "I've spent much time explaining the Gospel with a married woman on board. Should I continue?"

Herr Spangenberg was startled. "I would not advise you to give her up, but to talk so much to a married woman may be dangerous." He was shaking his finger.

The very next day John spent hours with Beata Hawkins again and in disgust recorded in his diary, "With Mrs. Hawkins too long, therefore did nothing."

Perhaps the noble Indians would take his mind off his unhealthy endeavor with Mrs. Hawkins. A contingent of the Yamacraw tribe soon came aboard. The ancient chief Tomochichi and John talked through the interpreter Mrs. Mary Musgrove, herself half Indian. Her English husband had drank himself to death. Now Mary ran a small trading post west of Savannah near the Yamacraws, who also were called the Lower Creeks.

Tomochichi said, "I am glad you are come. When I was in England, I desired that some would speak the Great Word to me and my nation. But we would not be made Christians as the Spanish make Christians. We would be taught before we are baptized."

"We would never force Christianity on a nonbeliever as the Spanish do," John replied. "Of course you must be taught. . . ."

Tomochichi's openness was a symphony to John's ears. Yes, that childlike wisdom was why he was here.

A few days later, the four Oxford men were being rowed up the Savannah River to visit the Yamacraws. The river was bounded by thick forests, appearing almost impenetrable because of vines webbed among the trees. The first clearing John saw was the public nursery on the east side of Savannah, already planted with grape vines, medical herbs, cotton and even flora doubtful for the climate, like cocoa beans and coffee shrubs. Also evident were many varieties of trees: mulberry to nourish silk worms, orange, apple, pear, olive and fig.

"I begin to appreciate the scope of James Oglethorpe's planning," John told Charles.

Savannah was divided meticulously into fenced lots fifty feet wide and ninety feet deep. Many houses were the original 24-by-16-foot unplaned wooden structures. But indicating just how prosperous the future would be for the town, more than a hundred new houses were in view, built of planed wood and painted white. Hugging the river was a small fortress with thick walls and twenty cannons.

"Not so obvious are the five-acre gardens and more distant forty-five-acre farms each male immigrant receives from Oglethorpe," John told Charles.

They went on to Cowpen, where Mary Musgrove informed John that Chief Tomochichi was not available just then. So the men returned to walk through Savannah. There at the small clapboard courthouse, which was also the church, John met the man he was to replace, Samuel Quincy. He also met a man of great influence in Savannah, Thomas Causton, who was not only the public store keeper but also first bailiff, or magistrate. John also saw the Moravians. But it was not Causton or the Moravians the Oxford men discussed as they returned to the *Simmonds*.

"Quincy seems a very amiable and able man to me," John commented.

"I heard it said he left Savannah for six months to go visit the English settlements in New England," Delamotte said.

"Yes," John mulled, "Oglethorpe would consider that abandoning your duty."

"What could motivate a conscientious man to do that?" Charles wondered in a worried voice.

Back at the *Simmonds,* John once again ministered to Beata Hawkins. He was drawn to her like a moth to a flame. Her attraction astonished and confused him. Was he being drawn in by a married woman? Herr Spangenberg was certainly concerned. Much to his relief, Mrs. Hawkins and her husband, as well as the Welches and some others, soon would be going to Frederica, a new settlement eighty sand-slogged miles south of Savannah. Frederica also could be reached by sea because it was on the inland side of the St. Simon Island that faced the Atlantic. Unspoken was the fact that it would be the southernmost English settlement in America—the first line of defense against the Spanish who were settled farther south in Florida.

Although John was relieved to see Mrs. Hawkins leave, he was not relieved to see Charles go, too. Oglethorpe would be in Frederica overseeing its development, so naturally his secretary Charles would be there. Ingham went to Frederica as well.

John returned to Cowpen to select a site for a schoolhouse for the Yamacraws. On March 7, 1736, he preached his first sermon in Savannah. Nearly one hundred crowded the church. The vast majority of these families were headed by failed tradesmen: bakers, cobblers, carpenters, barbers, butchers, bricklayers and laborers. Someone had told John these parishioners would be as well dressed as if they were in London. John had doubted. After all, most of these people were saved from debtors' prison. But soon he no longer doubted.

"They do appear quite prosperous," he told Delamotte.

John himself was in no simple frock. He wore a long, black cassock overlain by the white, ankle-length surplice. Two hard-starched white collars banded his neck. Today he even wore a thin black scarf over his soldiers—the mark of his master's degree. A white wig of tight curls flowed to his shoulders. He rarely wore a wig but today felt he had to meet his flock in full ecclesiastical splendor.

John opened the service with a list of hard and fast rules that were upheld in the Anglican High Church everywhere. "Number one: I must admonish you, not only in public, but from house to house. Two: I can admit none to Holy Communion without previous notice. Three: I shall divide the morning service on Sunday as designed by the church. Four: I must obey the rubric by dipping all children for baptism who are able to endure it. Five: I can admit none who are not communicants to be sponsors in baptism."

He paused and went on. "Six: I am only a servant of the Church of England, not a judge, and therefore I am obliged to keep her regulations in all things." This last, he hoped, would explain his minister's role, hard though it may be, as clearly as possible.

Was it his imagination that each time he went on to a new rule, the faces in the congregation hardened a bit more? Surely it was. All he had stated was the stark minimum for discipline. He shook off the uneasy feeling. Love filled his voice as he preached on Paul's great message of love in First Corinthians 13.

Later, he asked Delamotte uncertainly, "As you studied the faces of the worshipers in church, did you detect a high degree of attentiveness and respect?"

"They seem most agreeable and receptive," Delamotte replied.

"Do you think my opening rubrics too abrupt?"

"We shall see," Delamotte answered cautiously.

From Samuel Quincy, John learned to his surprise that his mission was not to evangelize the Indians yet. But how then had John gotten that impression? Was it mere puffery, to get the support of well-meaning people back in England for this new colony? Moreover, Quincy insisted that in spite of what Tomochichi said, the adult Yamacraws would never listen.

John might reach the young ones in the school, but not the older ones. John's duty was to the English settlers, Quincy said.

And John needn't bother Oglethorpe about it, either, he insisted. "We must not irritate the Indians," Quincy cautioned. "Otherwise, they might very well go over to help the French. You must never forget that we English are vying with the French and Spanish for this new continent of America."

"But I'm here to live with the Indians," John protested weakly.

On March 15, Quincy departed and John moved into the parsonage. It was the largest house in town, so it could accommodate visitors. Somewhat stunned at the latest revelation about his duties, John inventoried the many books in the parsonage. Bibles, psalters and common prayer books were there by the dozen, as well as works by Josephus, Plato and others.

Next, John set out to meet all seven hundred of his parishioners, just as his father would have done. On March 13, he met two young women. They were so attractive they frightened him, yet they badly needed instruction. Neither young lady was married. Neither was yet twenty. Elizabeth Fosset was most pleasant. Sophy Hopkey was breathtaking.

His mind was in turmoil. He had just rid himself of the temptation of Beata Hawkins. Did he dare suggest private lessons for these two comely maidens? In a letter to Charles in Frederica, he added in Greek—to thwart prying eyes: "I stand in jeopardy every hour. Two or three are women, younger, refined, God-fearing. Pray that I know none of them after the flesh."

John felt sick. He had thought America would free him of such torment. . . .

seven

Indecision

S ophy Hopkey was the niece of Thomas Causton. Although John was more aware than ever of the dangerous line between pastorly concern and lust, he began instructing Sophy and Elizabeth every morning. He assured himself the half hour he spent with them was but a small part of his very busy day. After all, he rose at four and worked steadily until ten at night. He prayed with Delamotte and sang hymns with the Moravians before he gave the morning prayer service in the church. From twelve to three, the time the settlers considered too hot to work, he visited their homes. The rest of the day he worked in his garden, prayed, wrote letters and gave the evening prayer service. He was even compiling a hymnal. His day was very full. Couldn't he spare a few moments every morning to instruct a couple of young ladies? "Am I to deny them the Gospel?" he asked himself.

On March 30, Ingham came from Frederica with astonishing news. "Charles is in all kinds of trouble there, John. You must go to him at once." Ingham's account of what happened was too preposterous for John to believe. Surely Ingham was suffering from hysteria. What really had occurred?

Ingham stayed in Savannah so both John and Delamotte could go to Frederica. When John finally reached Frederica, he found Charles very sick. He had been denied rations by the store keeper. He was sleeping on the floor. Worst of all, he was heartsick. Weak as Charles was, he insisted John help him walk into the woods where they could speak privately.

"The entire settlement is up in arms at me," Charles said when at last they were alone. "First, Ingham and I angered the settlers by insisting they must not hunt on Sundays. It is sport. It is not allowed by the Church of England. You know that, John. Well, they were outraged, pointing out that all week long they worked incessantly, building the settlement. How were they to get fresh meat if they could not hunt on Sunday? So I took it to Oglethorpe. He supported me—most reluctantly—and made other arrangements to get fresh meat."

"Is that all? Surely reasonable men can work this problem out. . . ."

"It's a mere crumb to the seven-layer cake that fell since then. Ann Welch and Beata Hawkins were quarreling with each other. I put myself in the middle as peacemaker. Privately to me they both made the incredible claim that the other was immorally involved with James Oglethorpe. In short, my attempts to straighten this out and get to the truth were a disaster. The women spread lies about me regarding the same immoral behavior. Now even Oglethorpe has abandoned me."

John set to work at once. Every waking hour he talked to James Oglethorpe and Beata Hawkins and Ann Welch and all others involved. He persisted for five days. He discovered the two women, in spite of their quarreling, had conspired to destroy Charles's reputation. Charles's stern presence was not wanted in Frederica. Resentment at his righteous correction hung in the air as thick as smoke. How well John knew that hatred. His father had suffered it for almost fifty years.

John remained as calm as Charles was perturbed, and he smoothed feelings over, person by person. Miraculously, the situation began to heal.

Oglethorpe sighed. "We will let bygones be bygones."

Soon John and Delamotte left for Savannah. But John had the feeling Frederica had little goodwill left for Charles. And Oglethorpe, though tolerant, had no enthusiasm left for Charles, either. Charles's days there were numbered. And the behavior of Beata and Ann dumbfounded John. In all his days, he had never met such conniving, evil women. And he had spent many hours with Beata. Was she several women in one? Or was it possible Ann was the major villain?

Back in Savannah, John and Delamotte lamented the absence of their beloved Holy Club. Could they distill the best of these hundreds of settlers into another Holy Club? They would attempt to enlist a few of the most devout to meet once or twice a week. Then from that group they would select the crème de la crème. How John missed his old Holy Club discussions with other high-minded Anglicans.

John was not long back in Savannah when Charles was sent there by Oglethorpe. Now Frederica had no pastor. John and Ingham would alternate going there to minister. John went first to Frederica and persuaded Oglethorpe to send for Sophy and Elizabeth. Sophy had confided in him that she was uncomfortable in her uncle's house, so John felt no guilt about interfering with the family. Besides, their instruction should continue uninterrupted.

In Frederica, William Horton was so cold to John now that John confronted him. "What bothers you, Brother Horton?"

"I like nothing you do," he snarled. "All your sermons are satires upon certain persons, therefore I will never hear you more. And all the people are of like mind, for we won't hear ourselves abused."

So there it was again. How the sinners hated righteousness. How they hated correction. Those who hate the Light will hate him who labors to shine it on them.

But John was not really in America to correct the settlers,

anyway. He had not given up his main reason for leaving England. Several weeks later in Savannah he broached what he had been told was a delicate subject with Oglethorpe.

"It is my understanding, sir, that the Choctaws are a very unspoiled tribe. I wish to go among them and teach them the Gospel."

Oglethorpe paled. "I'll give you two reasons why you must not. First, the French will find you there and kill you. Secondly, you are needed here. Is there not sin enough for you here among the English?"

So Quincy had been right. James Oglethorpe wanted no one "meddling" with his friendly Indians. What could John do worthwhile in America then but attend to the settlers?

A few days later, in the cool dawn, John was swimming in the river with Charles and Delamotte. It was July and the days were hot. John and Charles had left the water to dry off. As Delamotte swam to shore he was followed by a huge, dark shape. As he emerged from the river, the water behind him exploded into white froth and the ghostly shape disappeared.

"What was that?" asked the bewildered Delamotte.

"A large alligator, perhaps?" John said dryly.

Delamotte laughed.

Charles cleared his throat. "Thank God I'm soon going back to England."

Oglethorpe made Charles a courier for important papers to England for the Crown. That way, Charles saved some face; it didn't seem he had been run out of Georgia.

In a small sailboat on the way to Charleston, John and Charles were hit by a storm in St. Helena's sound. The mast on their boat snapped in the gale. John clutched the rail, ready to jump overboard any second, if need be, and thrash alone through the waves.

They made it safely to shore. Once again John was angry

with himself, for he knew he was not ready for death. "Death does have a terrible sting," he muttered to himself.

In Charleston, John left a manuscript with printer Lewis Timothy. Soon, parishioners would be singing from the Wesley brothers' first hymnal, *Psalms and Hymns for Sunday.*

After Charles embarked July 26, 1736, John rushed south to Frederica. How long had it been since he had seen Sophy? But he walked straight into a quarrel. Apparently, a letter from Charles to John had been found by Dr. Hawkins. As usual, Charles had added a few caustic comments in Greek. But this time, the Greek had not been observed by just one person in a blink of an eye; it had been seen by dozens over a period of days, because the suspicious Hawkins had made it public. Even the settlers in Frederica could decipher Greek, if they had enough time. Charles had lambasted "women of Frederica."

Beata Hawkins confronted John. "Just which women do those scurrilous words describe? All the women in Frederica?"

"By no means. Just you and Ann Welch," John replied honestly.

"You miserable wretch, you scoundrel, you pitiful fool. . . ."

John excused himself. Later he was summoned by Beata. Perhaps she'd had a change of heart. He wasn't going to give up on her. Wasn't his mission in life to save souls? Cautiously he went to her house. Beata invited him inside and asked him to sit down. Then she stood in front of him with her arms behind her back.

"Sir, you have wronged me," she said. Her arm swung around to brandish a pistol!

John grabbed her arm. Her other arm swung around. She

thrust at him with a pair of scissors! He intercepted that arm. Now he held both her arms. They wrestled over the weapons. A maid came in, frantic as to what to do. A house boy entered, not knowing who to help, then ran out. The two combatants struggled. Finally a constable stormed in. By that time the ferocious Beata had sunk her teeth in John's cassock, ripping off both sleeves. After the constable had pulled her loose, John examined the pistol.

"Yes, it is loaded," he gasped. Sickened, he left the house.

In the days that followed, Dr. Hawkins and Beata spread lies about John attacking Beata. John had to go to James Oglethorpe to demand a trial. How else could he clear his name? Surely such an outrage would reach England. And he, of all people, the one who fled all flesh, would be portrayed a despicable lecher.

"This is a bad time for a trial, sir," Oglethorpe said wearily. "Of course, the publicity for the colony is very detrimental. But we also have a delegation of Spaniards coming to try to negotiate the boundary between their realm to the south and ours. I need time to prepare. And I need you, John, to act as my recorder. These negotiations must be recorded letter-perfect. I know how methodical you are."

"I would never harm the Crown, sir."

So Oglethorpe sat, reconciling John and the Hawkinses for hours and hours. Finally he got both sides to agree to maintain utter silence on the matter, as well as to never speak to each other again. John was satisfied, under the difficult circumstances.

After the turmoil ended, he began to see Sophy as much as four times a day. Once a day was not nearly enough for her instruction. Sometimes they accidentally touched, and the contact electrified him. He learned from her the tale of Tommy Mellichamp. The young criminal, in jail in

Savannah, supposedly had designs on Sophy. He had told the poor girl he would kill anyone who married her. And she believed him. She swore she could never marry.

But when John visited Savannah after the Spanish delegation had left Frederica, Sophy's uncle scoffed at the story of Mellichamp. "Nonsense. But she does need a suitor. Let him be but an honest, good man." He looked at John very directly. "I don't care whether he has a shilling. I can give him maintenance. I now own three houses. And Sophy has a dowry of her own."

John said nothing to commit himself, and when he returned to Frederica he made no marriage offer.

Causton didn't understand his resolve not to marry. And John was not obligated to tell him. He continued to see Sophy day after day. But she was changing. For months on end she had been quiet and pleasant. Now she seemed edgy. She began to talk of going back to England. When John married her friend Elizabeth Fosset to Welles Westen, Sophy became even more irritable and restless.

"Miss Sophy seems disturbed here," Oglethorpe said one day. "I wish her to return to her uncle in Savannah."

Only John could be trusted with the task, Oglethorpe said. John thought it was a blatant effort at matchmaking, yet he found it irresistible. For several days, he and Sophy traveled and talked. In his heart John longed for her. He acknowledged the desire now. It ate at him. Yet he had to shrink from her. Over and over in his mind he chanted Saint Paul's instructions to the believers at Corinth: *Are you unmarried? Do not look for a wife.* What if John were to marry? Could he ignore Saint Paul's further instructions? *Time is short. From now on those who have wives should live as if they had none.* So why be so unfair to a woman as to marry her? And religious matters aside, what about the miserable marriages his sisters had made?

But back in Savannah he couldn't stay away from Sophy. He set a schedule for her that required her to come to his house for breakfast and devotions, then French from eight to nine, and back again in the evening for reading and psalms. He ached for her. Yet he agonized over his weakness. In December, he listed more resolutions in a life already regimented to the minute:

1. *Be more watchful, before and in prayer.*
2. *Strive to be thankful in eating.*
3. *Not to touch even her clothes by choice; think not of her.*
4. *Every hour, have I prayed quite sincerely? Pray that you may watch, strive.*
5. *Look into no book but the Bible till Christmas.*
6. *From 12 to 4 o'clock, meditation or parish, no writing or reading.*

In January 1737, Tommy Mellichamp got out of jail. John fretted more than ever. He asked a Moravian friend if he might not weaken and think of marriage if he continued to associate with Sophy.

The Moravian was astonished, saying, "I don't see why you shouldn't marry!"

John couldn't be persuaded to marry. Yet he longed for Sophy constantly. In agony he sent her a note:

> *I find, Miss Sophy, I can't take fire into my bosom and not be burnt. I am therefore retiring for a while to desire the direction of God. Join with me, my friend, in fervent prayer, that He would show me what is best to be done.*

He struck off for the Indian schoolhouse of the Yama-craws, where he stayed a while. When he wasn't praying, he furiously chopped wood and caulked a boat. And he heard no direction from God. He went back to Savannah by boat for one hour, but left again. In his diary that day he wrote hot words:

> . . . .*Again I felt, and groaned under the weight of, an unholy desire. My heart was with Miss Sophy all the time. I longed to see her, were it but for a moment. And when I was called to [embark again], it was as the sentence of death; but believing it was the call of God, I obeyed. I walked awhile to and fro on the edge of the water, heavy laden and pierced through with many sorrows.*

He returned to Savannah later, still in torment. He was drawn to Sophy immediately. Now Sophy was dropping hints of marriage. There was no longer any doubt why she was irritable. She was tired of waiting. Her aunt dropped hints, too. Her uncle dropped hints. When was John going to do something? Why was he spending so much time with Sophy if he had no intentions of marriage?

One day a settler screamed, "The Spaniards are coming!"

The rumor of an invasion by Spaniards seemed to snap John out of his lovesick denial. Oglethorpe was back in England. The Spaniards had certainly picked the right time to attack.

Bailiff Causton sent men around Savannah making a list of able-bodied men to fight the Spaniards. The Moravians refused to cooperate. Oglethorpe had promised to honor their pacifist ideals and never conscript them for military duty. The

English in the town became angry.

A mob taunted the Moravians. "Why can't you Moravians fight for the women and children?" they screamed.

The Moravians calmly replied they would pick up and leave Savannah. Causton was shaken. Oglethorpe would be very angry about that; he liked the Moravians. The Moravians worked very hard and never made trouble.

John discussed the injustice to the Moravians with Delamotte and Ingham. One of them had to sail for England immediately and appraise Oglethorpe. It was decided Ingham would go.

Days after Ingham left for England, it became apparent the Spaniards were not going to attack. The situation calmed. John began to fret over Sophy again. Finally, in early March, he discussed with Delamotte what he should do. "I've waited too long for this meeting already," John said. "Ingham should have voted on this issue, too."

"We know that Ingham is strongly opposed to your marrying Sophy," Delamotte said calmly. "And I feel if you continue to see Sophy you must marry her."

John sighed. "And my heart says wait, wait, wait." He was shocked to hear himself say that. Had he come that far?

"Three votes. And three different opinions," Delamotte said. "We Oxford men made a pact that if there was no majority decision, lots would be cast. . . ."

"But is this such an occasion?" John asked.

"Consider this," Delamotte said. "One lot for Ingham is 'Think of marriage no more.' One lot for me is 'Marry.' One lot for you is 'Wait.' "

John wrote those words on three slips of paper and put them in a hat. "Now let the Searcher of hearts decide," he implored God.

Delamotte reached in, pulled out a slip and read, "Think of marriage no more."

It was the answer John's head wanted. But he felt like he had been slapped in the face. His heart was sick and angry. What had he done? He had refused such a companion as he never expected to find again, should he live one thousand years twice over. Yet he must not weaken. The lots had been cast. He must tell Sophy right away that he could never marry.

Yet over the next few days he didn't tell her. He continued to see her again and again, while dodging every opportunity for discussion of marriage blatantly thrown his way by Sophy and her family.

One morning John was met at the door by Sophy's aunt. She looked triumphant.

"We are exceedingly obliged for all the pains you've taken about Sophy," she said vacantly. "So is Sophy. Now she desires you publish the banns of her marriage to Mr. William Williamson."

John almost fainted. Wasn't Williamson a mere lodger at their house? How had this happened? The man didn't even attend prayer meetings. Yet at last it was done. For months and months, John had played around the edge of the abyss. Now his torment was over.

But was it? In his diary that day, he recorded his hourly confusion and heartbreak. He could think of nothing else. He couldn't blot Sophy out even from his prayers. His last entry of the day was:

> *No such day since I first saw the sun!*
> *Oh deal tenderly with Thy servant!*
> *Let me not see such another!*

In the next days, he discovered it was not over. He could not get Sophy out of his mind. He could not rid himself of the pain in his heart. What would he have done if he had known he would suffer such agony over losing Sophy? He was not at all proud of his celibacy now. He felt wretched. He had never felt worse in his entire life. He knew now he had made a terrible mistake. And now the situation was hopeless for him.

"Or is there hope?" he suddenly asked himself.

He began to think he should oppose the marriage. Wasn't he the pastor? Yes, this Williamson was definitely not fit for Sophy. It was John's duty as pastor to prevent a bad marriage. But would that seem sour and petty to everyone? On the other hand, had his father Samuel ever flinched from his duty? Certainly not.

But still John couldn't make up his mind. Yes, he would stop it. No, he must not stop it. Yes, he must stop it. . . .

Delamotte interrupted his vacillations. "It seems Mr. Williamson took Miss Sophy over to Purrysburg, South Carolina, to be married." He shrugged. "They were married in the Church of England"—as if that settled it once and for all.

"But wait," John snapped. "The banns have not been published yet! I can still get the marriage annulled."

But he didn't. Annulling it would really seem sour and petty. He fumed over it, though. It was not a righteous marriage. He should have prevented it.

He pored over his diary that night. What! Could this be? Yes, it was true. Sophy was married one year to the day after John first had met her on March 13, 1736!

Later, he indulged his anger by complaining to the bishop about the marriage being performed before the banns were published. He told Delamotte he was considering refusing her Holy Communion. John saw a look in Delamotte's eyes he had never seen before: deep disappointment. *Delamotte was young*, John thought. Some day he would understand John had to perform his duties, whether it made him look spiteful or not. He could not shirk his duty. . . .

So John began a battle with Sophy and the Caustons about her religious duties. After all, he had instructed her. Was Sophy at services often enough? Was she fasting? Had she given previous notice she wanted Holy Communion? Finally, in July, he wrote her a letter:

> *Would you [like to] know what I dislike in your past or present behavior? You have always heard my thoughts as freely as you asked them. Nay, much more freely; you know it well, and so you shall do, as long as I can speak or write. In your present behavior I dislike (1) your neglect of half the public service, which no man living can compel you to; (2) your neglect of fasting, which you once knew to be a help to the mind, without any prejudice to the body; (3) your neglect of almost half the opportunity of [Holy Communion] which you lately had. But these things are small in comparison of what I dislike in your past. . . .*

Then John wrote of all his grievances in their relationship. He knew it would probably be misconstrued. He considered their relationship spiritual, even if others considered it courtship—and inept, at that. But he couldn't help himself. He had a duty as her pastor. The battle wasn't over.

In early August, his words were ominous to his old Moravian friend August Spangenberg. He said, "The calm we have so long enjoyed is drawing to an end. You will shortly see that I am not, as some might have told you, a respecter of persons.

I am determined, God being my helper, to behave indifferently to all, rich or poor, friends or enemies."

On August 7, when Sophy knelt at the rail in church, John refused to give her Holy Communion!

eight

The Internal Witness

The Caustons were humiliated, then furious. The very next day, a complaint was issued against John for defaming Sophy Williamson. The anger in the community grew at what seemed sour revenge by a bumbling suitor. Magistrate Causton called a grand jury and gave them a list of grievances against John:

1. *Speaking and writing to Mrs. Williamson without her husband's consent.*
2. *Repelling her from Holy Communion.*
3. *Not declaring his adherence to the Church of England.*
4. *Dividing the morning service on Sundays.*
5. *Refusing to baptize Mr. Parker's child, otherwise than by dipping, except the parents would certify it was weak, and not able to bear it.*
6. *Repelling William Gough from the Holy Communion.*
7. *Refusing to read the burial service over the body of Nathaniel Polhill.*

And the list went on. John remained calm. He could not argue with the veracity of the list. But he had merely enforced the rubrics of the church. Perhaps Savannah was not ready for the High Church of England. Still, John was willing to explain himself. He respected the law. And after all, he was in the right. Everything he had done was in his jurisdiction as cleric of the Church of England.

But he found himself appearing again and again in court, answering complaints. It became obvious the suits were now a form of harassment by Causton. John could get no work done. So he stopped answering summonses for court appearances. When he heard the chaplain at Frederica had been ordered to come to Savannah to hold services for those who could not tolerate John, he began to see the handwriting on the wall.

Delamotte was blunt. "It looks grim, John."

Some of his friends advised him to go back to England. John refused. He would fight it out here in America. But then he was ordered to post bail or go to jail. Bail was an enormous sum: fifty pounds. That was more than John's entire budget for the church for one year! John knew then he had to leave. With James Oglethorpe still in England, he would not get justice in America. Causton was too powerful and too adept at legal maneuvering. John might actually waste away in jail. But still he hesitated to leave. He would look like a criminal.

"Leave right away, John!" Delamotte urged one day. "Causton has issued an order for your arrest. He heard you might be preparing to leave. He is determined to bring you to your knees—to imprison you, to impoverish you. All law officers in Georgia are being advised to prevent John Wesley from leaving the colony!"

On the dark night of December 3, 1737, John Wesley, minister of the Church of England, Oxford fellow, fled Georgia on foot. In South Carolina at Charleston, he boarded the *Samuel*.

The voyage back to England was the darkest moment yet

of John's life. Nothing seemed to cheer him. Though the injustice of Georgia faded, John's failure grew. What else could it be called?

Each hour the failure grew larger and more tender, like an angry boil. Even as Sophy's loss diminished, a more bitter realization loomed and grew. John had lost his faith!

On January 8, 1738, he wrote:

> *By the most infallible of proofs, inward feeling,*
> *I am convinced:*
> 1. *Of unbelief, having no such faith in Jesus Christ*
>   *as will prevent my heart from being troubled;*
>   *which it could not be, if I believed in God and*
>   *rightly believed also in Him.*
> 2. *Of pride, throughout my life past; inasmuch I*
>   *thought I had what I find I have not.*
> 3. *Of gross irrecollection; in as much in a storm I*
>   *cried to God every moment; in a calm, not.*
> 4. *Of levity and luxuriancy of spirit, recurring when*
>   *ever the pressure is taken off.*

After two more weeks of torment and praying, his faith had not been restored. But it had been tested again. The ship had nearly gone down in mountain-high seas during a storm on Friday the 13th of January. Depressed, he wrote:

> *I went to America to convert the Indians; but*
> *O! who shall convert me? Who, what is he*
> *that will deliver me from this evil heart of mis-*
> *chief? I have a fair summer of religion. I can*
> *talk well; nay, and believe myself, while no*
> *danger is near; but let death look me in the*
> *face, and my spirit is troubled. Nor can I say,*

"To die is gain!. . . .In a storm I think, "What if the Gospel be not true?" (Then I am of all men most foolish). . . .A wise man advised me some time since, "Be still and go on." Perhaps this is best; to look upon it as my cross. . . .

The *Samuel* neared England toward the end of January. The voyage had been a very fast one, with but the one bad storm. Yet the voyage had seemed an eternity in hell for John. With England in sight, he recorded:

It is now almost two years and almost four months since I left my native country, in order to teach the Georgia Indians the nature of Christianity. But what have I learned in the meantime? Why, what I least of all suspected, that I, who went to America to convert others, was never myself converted to God.

Then, paraphrasing Saint Paul's immortal lament in Second Corinthians 11, John wrote:

"I am not mad," though I thus speak; but "I speak the words of truth and soberness"; if haply some of those who still dream may awake and see that as I am, so are they. Are they read in philosophy? So was I. In ancient or modern tongues? So was I also. Are they versed in the science of divinity? I too have studied it many years. Can they talk fluently upon spiritual things? The very same I could do. Are they plenteous in alms? "Behold I gave all my goods to feed the poor." Do they

*give of their labor as well as of their sub-
stance? I have labored more abundantly than
they all. Are they willing to suffer for their
brethren? I have thrown up my friends, reputation, ease, country; I have put my life in my
hands, wandering into strange lands; I have
given my body to be devoured by the deep,
parched up by heat, consumed with toil and
weariness, or whatsoever God should bring
upon me. But does all this—be it more or less,
it matters not—make me acceptable to God?
Does all I ever did or can know, say, give, do
or suffer, justify me in His sight? . . . "I am
fallen short of the glory of God.". . . I am "a
child of wrath" and heir to hell. . . .*

At Dover he stayed overnight at an inn, learning that
friend George Whitefield had just embarked for Georgia.
John probably had seen the billowing sails of his ship.

In his room he tried to justify the last two years in America.
Surely there were some accomplishments. He had learned
piety and real moral courage from the Moravians. He had
learned to read German and Spanish.

Surely there must be other accomplishments. He had con-
firmed the worth of casting lots. Hadn't that saved him from
Sophy? That last assertion turned very sour in his mouth.

The next day, he journeyed on to London, very depressed.
How would he be received? What news had preceded him?
What would Oglethorpe say to him?

John's first social call was at Delamotte's Blendon Hall
near Bexley. If these old friends were cool to him, London
would be icy indeed.

But they treated him like their long-lost son. "Praise God

for that warmth," he said after he left the Delamottes.

Hours later, John joined brother Charles once again at James Hutton's home in Westminster. There seemed no antagonism or anxiety whatever over Georgia. Apparently, the news about the colonies had been well-controlled by the Crown. The Hutton family wanted to know even less than what everyone usually wanted to know from returned travelers. "Charles has already described America from flora to fauna to Choctaw," James Hutton explained.

Later, when the brothers were alone, John heard all the news of their family, then of England. King George was quarreling with his son Prince Frederick. Queen Caroline had died, but her protégé, Robert Walpole, virtually ran the government. John also learned Charles had been reflecting on his own failure in America for a long time.

Charles said, "I repeated our own dear father's failure at Epworth and Wroot. He was so conscientious about the sins of his flock he earned their hardy dislike, but the poor man was too busy and ungracious to earn their affection."

John shook his head. "Precisely, Charles. And I seem to have gone on to repeat it yet again." John went into his long tale of woe in Savannah. Finally, he said, "Yes, I failed, but I'm sure it was also a failure of the flock. Must we ignore their sins? No, I don't think so." He paused and girded himself. "What is the disposition of James Oglethorpe these days?"

"Mainly he is worried that you might portray the settlers as unworthies and cause his Georgia colony to lose the support of the English."

"I'll see him at the earliest opportunity to reassure him I'll do nothing of the sort."

To his surprise, John found he was in demand as a preacher around London. People hungered for news abut the "New World." And John hungered to preach to Londoners. Surely these high-bred High Church English would not be offended by John's demands for spiritual perfection.

At St. John the Evangelist's church he preached very strongly on Paul's message in Second Corinthians 5: *Therefore, if anyone is in Christ, he is a new creation; the old has gone, the new has come!* After the service, the pastor informed John that many of the best sort in the congregation were very offended. What was John hinting at? "Surely such stalwarts as they don't need to change," the pastor insisted. "Pray, don't plan on preaching here again, sir."

A Dutch merchant contacted John to tell him a group of Moravians from Germany were in London for a while before sailing to America. John not only met them, speaking the German he had learned from the Moravians in Georgia, but found them lodging near the Huttons. He planned on talking to them at every opportunity, especially to one sunny individual named Peter Boehler. Peter's face glowed with living faith.

How John admired the Moravians. Someday, somehow, he must have the inner spiritual peace they had.

The next Sunday, he preached at St. Andrew's in Holborn on First Corinthians 13: *If I give all I possess to the poor and surrender my body to the flames, but have not love, I gain nothing.* Here, too, the pastor was alarmed after the service. He had seen the anger flare in the faces of his flock. Why was John so hard on them? They were good people. They harmed no one. It really would be best if John didn't preach there again.

John spoke often with Peter Boehler over the next days. "How is it you have such spiritual peace?" John asked him in German, for Peter knew almost no English.

Peter could not explain how. No matter how John tried to coax it out of him through sound steps of logic, Peter could not explain it. Finally, Peter snapped, "My brother, that philosophy of yours must be purged away!"

"I don't understand."

"Exactly, brother! The peace of God transcends all understanding."

But to John that was too mystical. And he labored over resolutions to achieve spiritual perfection. He listed four he was sure would help:

1. *be absolutely frank and unreserved with everyone;*
2. *achieve continual seriousness, uninterrupted by the slightest trace of levity;*
3. *speak only of the glory of God, never of worldly things; and*
4. *take no pleasure that does not contribute to the glory of God.*

John finally saw his mother Susanna at Salisbury. She was staying with Patty. Susanna praised the hospitality of Westley Hall, and Patty was cheerful, but John discovered the oily Hall was philandering.

Of his other five sisters, he already had learned Emily was still unhappy, her husband a broken man. Sukey had left her husband to drift among her grown children. Hetty had lived with Uncle Matthew in London until he died in June 1737; now she reconciled with her drunken husband off and on. Only Anne in Hatfield seemed unscathed by marriage. Kezzy was a searching, spiritual spinster in the home of Rev. Piers at Bexley.

After John went to Tiverton to see Sammy, he received word that Charles was at Oxford, dying! He rushed there immediately. Charles was suffering a severe attack of pleurisy. They had bled him and poured all sorts of elixirs into him. For four days it appeared he was going to die. Then he began to recover. Peter Boehler was there with him, too. Once again John was struck by the peace Peter had. Suddenly John had a complete collapse of faith.

"Brother Boehler, how can I preach to others of faith," he asked privately, "if I have none myself?"

"Preach faith until you have it. And then because you have it, you will continue to preach faith."

So John continued to preach. And his message was hard. He rarely ever was invited back. One by one he was eliminating every pulpit in the London and Oxford areas. What was to become of him?

Meanwhile, he sought spiritual advice from Boehler. He could not have such conversations with Charles, who was still sick but now back at Hutton's. In the past when he had told Charles of his wavering faith, Charles had become livid. It was just too much of a disappointment for him.

Peter insisted someday John would find what he was looking for. It would be instantaneous. John would not be able to explain afterward what had happened.

But John was a skeptic. Did that explanation bear examination? He searched the New Testament. Indeed, there were many sudden transformations. Oh, the Moravians were so wise. Peter was but a young man, perhaps ten years younger than John. Yet he was so wise.

But in the meantime, faith eluded John. He was sure he no longer had it. Perhaps he would be inspired by the new society begun in London at Fetter Lane on May 1, 1738, by James Hutton. At Peter's urging, it was founded on the word of God from James 5:16:

> *Therefore confess your sins to each other*
> *and pray for each other so that you may be*

healed. The prayer of a righteous man is powerful and effective.

It was very nearly in the image of their Holy Club at Oxford, but there was one striking difference: it was not elitist. This was Peter's contribution. Of the nine original members, only John, Hutton and John Shaw were of the educated gentry. The others were all tradesmen and laborers!

John marveled to Charles about the laborer John Bray. "He knows nothing but Christ, yet by knowing Him, he knows and discerns all things."

"We've been too isolated, Brother. Wasn't the tinker John Bunyan even a more brilliant version of how a man who knows only the Word can know everything important?"

Still, John did not find that faith he was searching for.

Then Peter Boehler sailed for America. John became very depressed again. The month of May was not going well for him. Church after church told him not to preach to their congregations again: St. Catherine's, St. Lawrence's, St. Ann's at Aldersgate, St. John's at Wapping, St. Bennet's at Paul's Wharf, and on and on. John was not advancing the faith. He was sinking it.

And he became so angry in his search for faith he wrote a blistering, tactless letter to William Law:

> *Once more, sir, let me beg you to consider whether your extreme roughness, and morose and sour behavior, at least on many occasions, can possibly be the fruit of a living faith in Christ. . . .*

About this time Charles, still sick, claimed to have a sudden spiritual awakening. One of the Moravians, William Holland, came to his room and preached from Martin Luther's *Commentary on Galatians*. Later that night, Charles could not stop thinking about verses 20 and 21 in Galatians 2:

> *I have been crucified with Christ and I no longer live, but Christ lives in me. The life I live in the body, I live by faith in the Son of God, who loved me and gave himself for me. I do not set aside the grace of God, for if righteousness could be gained through the law, Christ died for nothing!*

Charles fell asleep praying, "If only it were true for me, Charles Wesley."

"And in the morning, John, my prayer was answered," Charles answered. "At last I have rest for my soul. I immediately began to feel healthier, too."

Three days later, John awoke and opened his Bible. He often considered the first thing he read as a message from God regarding his immediate circumstances. This morning it popped open to Second Peter 1:4:

> *. . . .He has given us His very great and precious promises, so that through them you may participate in the divine nature and escape the corruption in the world caused by evil desires.*

"If only that were to come true for me," John thought.

That evening he was supposed to go to a society meeting in Aldersgate. He did not want to go. He was very depressed. No one sought faith harder than he did, yet he was denied faith.

But he trudged to the meeting in Nettleton Court. There was that same William Holland, this time reading from Luther's *Preface to Romans*. John listened lifelessly. Holland reached the portion describing the change God works in the heart through faith in Christ. The heart, John reflected analytically, is Paul's euphemism for thought and feeling inside a person. It is neither righteous nor evil, but the inner place where the Spirit must dwell, if at all.

Suddenly, an inexplicable warmth swelled inside John's chest! His heart seemed to buoy him off the floor. His mind soared. He realized he did trust Christ alone for salvation. Christ had died for him, John Wesley. Christ's blood had washed away John Wesley's sins. Christ alone had saved John Wesley from death.

John, who always tried to note every detail, shakily noted the time that evening of May 24, 1738: it was eight-forty-five. He seemed a new man, reborn. While the meeting continued, John prayed for all those who had abused him: "Forgive them, God."

As the meeting was drawing to a close, he stood up and spoke with joy. "Friends, this evening I have felt the internal witness of the Spirit. On his deathbed, my father told me this must happen. The Moravians told me this must happen. And by God's grace it has happened inside me this very evening."

Later that evening he fought temptation after temptation. Each time he was tempted, he lifted his eyes to God and resisted. John was strong as he had never been strong before. He had power—and why not? It was one of the six gifts of the Holy Spirit the prophet Isaiah had revealed more than two thousand years before: wisdom, understanding, counsel, knowledge, fear of the Lord—and power. As he went to sleep that night, John was certain that whereas before he was sometimes conquered by temptation, now with the gifts of the Holy Spirit he would foil temptation—every time.

The next morning he awoke with "Jesus, Master" on his lips. "I am sure I am in Christ now, a new creation," he cried. "Life will never be the same. I am sure of that."

Theologically, he had not changed one iota. It was a matter of God's grace. He believed with all his heart and soul that Christ had saved him, John Wesley. And he began to shout it from the rooftops. Before May 24 he was not a Christian at all, he claimed. Now in his zeal he urged everyone to admit they were not Christians and seek this spiritual awakening.

That accusation was so shocking, James Hutton's mother wrote Sammy and urged him to take John in hand before he corrupted her children. John, she worried, was not quite right in the head.

But John was sure he was a new creation. Once again the Moravians had predicted what would happen. He had seen their dedicated community in Georgia. Now he must see at their source how they lived and applied the Gospel. That was the practice of holiness.

He arranged to go to Germany with three Moravians and four other Englishmen, one of whom was his old friend Ingham. "So many pulpits are closed to me around London I am sure I will not be missed," John told Charles.

Just three weeks after his spiritual awakening, he left for Germany. After traveling up the Rhine by boat, he met Count Zinzendorf at Marienborn. They had long theological discussions in Latin. From there John and the other pilgrims traveled to Herrnhut, thirty miles from Dresden. This was the model Moravian community. After that he visited their schools and orphan houses at Halle.

Yet in September, John returned to London disillusioned. In John's mind, the Moravians had fallen far short of holiness. The count had been too dictatorial. The Moravians had been too proud of their enterprise. Some were cunning. Some were connivers. Some were even liars.

John tried to sort it out. He must not condemn the effort because some Moravians had failed. Even some of the Lord's twelve had failed. Maybe John had not seen any Kingdom on earth established by these Moravians, but England certainly had nothing as noble as the Moravians' effort to apply their faith to living.

"Somehow I must use what I've learned, even though I'm almost an outcast in my own church," he puzzled to himself. "The Moravians had to leave the Lutheran Church. Is that what I must do to establish a living faith? Leave the Church of England?"

He recoiled from that. It seemed unthinkable.

nine

Field Preaching

By this time, John thought he had resolved the theological question of why his conversion years ago did not seem to bring the gifts of the Holy Spirit but required yet another step that glorious night in May. John wasn't the only one who had experienced this. Martin Luther had been tormented by the paradox. John Bunyan detailed his own torment in *Grace Abounding*. So the bewilderment was common. And those who persevered were rescued eventually from doubt.

"There must be a second work of grace from faith," John told Charles.

"That would explain it, if true."

"The first work of grace imputes righteousness; that is, it charges us with the responsibility of being righteous. The result is what Saint Paul calls justification. The second work of grace actually imparts righteousness. It causes in the recipient real holiness or sanctification. And the sanctified is aware of the presence of the Holy Spirit within."

"What father called 'the internal witness of the Spirit'? " Charles asked.

"Yes. I don't believe sanctification leads to spiritual perfection, because we all remain sinners. But at least, the one sanctified consciously, consistently rejects sin."

"So that the sanctification you describe is as complete as salvation gets in this world?"

"Yes. But it is not described by me, but Saint Paul in the 8th chapter of Romans," John answered.

"And so our good works flow naturally from sanctification as we put into practice holiness," Charles added.

Back in London, John threw himself into visiting jails and workhouses, as well as attending small society meetings. The society at Fetter Lane was particularly inviting. One of his most avid followers there was a young widow named Grace Murray. She seemed to yearn for spiritual growth. He was very attracted to her, but reminded himself that it had not been one year since his heart had been torn apart by Sophy Hopkey.

"She is sweet and gentle and humble, to be sure—just like Sophy," Charles said pointedly.

Now that John preached a doctrine of what most clerics considered mystical conversion, the pulpits became even more reluctant to have him. He and Charles were uncertain at this time whether to go back to Oxford. They carried on, not aimlessly but obscurely.

In March 1739, John received an invitation from George Whitefield to come to Bristol. Whitefield had been back from Georgia since December. He, too, found the pulpits in England closed to his hard message. Now he was doing the unthinkable.

"He is preaching outside of the church—literally," John said to Charles.

"But preaching among trees?" Charles asked, perturbed. "With the clods under his feet as his pulpit?"

"With the sky as his sounding board, Brother," John continued, just as uneasy.

"Surely you are not going. It's so unseemly." Impulsively, Charles grabbed a Bible. He, too, often accepted as God's will the first verse his eyes fell on when he opened the Bible at random. "Look here, John. Ezekiel 24:16."

They both read God's supposed message to Charles:

> *. . . .With one blow I am about to take away*
> *from you the delight of your eyes. Yet do not*
> *lament or weep or shed any tears.*

John's jaw dropped. "It seems you've sent me to Bristol, brother."

Charles searched John's face. "You don't want to go, do you? Consult the society at Fetters Lane."

No agreement could be reached at the society meeting on Fetter Lane. So lots were cast. The lot drawn urged John to Bristol. So he went in spite of his misgivings.

Trade with America had made Bristol the liveliest city in England, outside London. The city bustled with seafaring men, typically notorious sinners when in port. George Whitefield had been preaching there, as well as to the coal miners of nearby Kingswood. Now he wanted to return to America.

Whitefield got straight to the point. "I want you to carry on my work," he said.

"What! Preaching outdoors is repugnant to me," John said with his usual bluntness.

Whitefield smiled. "I'm sure what you say to me is true. When did you not speak the truth? But I also know you are a most reasonable man. So let me make my case."

"Proceed, brother," John said skeptically.

"Certain areas of England are booming as never before, John," Whitefield explained. "Now, here in Bristol it happens to be booming because of shipping and in Kingswood because of coal mining. But all over England certain local areas are exploding with new activity and growth. Jethro

Tull has revolutionized farming with his seed planters and other inventions. John Kay has revolutionized weaving with his flying shuttle. Machines are being invented for this and that, left and right."

"I'm beginning to see the problem. . . ."

"The Church of England is notoriously slow to create new parishes."

"Of course. It takes an act of Parliament."

"So you do see the dilemma, friend. Great enclaves of the unchurched are growing. The poorest laborers and farmers among us are unchurched. Someone must do something. And if you and I are not welcome in the pulpits of the churches, perhaps it is God's will that we reach the un-churched out of the pulpit."

"But are they interested?" John shook his head. "The unchurched—with no instruction, no background. They're heathen."

"Did you not once go to America to reach the red heathen?" asked Whitefield. "And were you not denied the opportunity? Friend, the opportunity is right here in England among the white heathen, a thousandfold!"

"Your argument is unassailable."

On April 1, Whitefield took John with him as he spoke to a gathering in the bowling green at Pithay in Bristol. A crowd gathered, many tittering nervously. The sight of a clergyman in his solemn tunics was so tantalizing, John thought. How could they not wonder what this cleric was going to do?

Within minutes, Whitefield had the crowd spellbound. He was like a great Shakespearean actor. Every crisp syllable off his tongue struck one's ears, one moment like the purr of a cat, the next moment like thunder. From experience, John knew Whitefield's voice carried far beyond the farthest listener. His every gesture was exaggerated. He spoke of being born again. The Church of England did not teach this from its pulpits, yet it was contained in the thirty-nine articles of the church. All men and women are under sin until released by their faith in Christ. Only that is sufficient. Good works are not sufficient.

Whitefield was the most dynamic preacher John had ever heard. Yet John was sickened by this outdoor preaching. First of all, he himself couldn't preach like Whitefield at all. And all his life, John had gained comfort from the trappings of the church. He was such a stickler for order. Everyone knew that. This field preaching seemed so crude. "Surely one could not save souls in a bowling green!" John muttered to himself.

Yet John felt compelled to go with Whitefield as he continued into the mine-pitted region of Kingswood, past slag heaps and pitiful shacks. They stopped at a place called Hannam Mount. From that green rise, Whitefield preached again, just as strongly. The crowd seemed hungry for the Word. Some obviously had heard Whitefield before.

The clerics continued across Kingswood to Rose Green. Again a crowd gathered, larger than the one before, to hear Whitefield preach.

John's head was spinning with the events of the day. How many thousands had Whitefield reached? And what poverty and misery infested Kingswood! What work there was to be done here! But could the heathen be reached?

That night, while Whitefield preached to a small society on Baldwin Street, John preached to a small society on Nicholas Street. John's message was hard, but unlike Whitefield's alternating purrs and thunder, his delivery was constantly graceful and easy. His voice was clear, almost conversational. Yet he knew it resonated off walls and ceilings. John was far too methodical not to have learned how to project his voice inside a building. Surely this safety of the enclosure was his destiny.

But Whitefield implored him to preach under the sky the next afternoon, at the brick yard at the end of Saint Phillip's Plain.

"Give it a chance," he urged John. "For I'm leaving for Gloucester tomorrow at dawn. Then I'll be in the London area until I sail again for America."

The next day—April 2, 1739—John trudged to the brick yard at four o'clock in the afternoon, feeling the fool, stumbling over clods in his elegant cassocks. But when he saw the crowd of grimy laborers and their families, his heart ached; they required his utmost effort. And now he realized the extent of the crowd. Thronged on the clay banks were at least three thousand people!

John stood on a small rise and preached on the very essence of his own calling, from Luke 4:18: *The Spirit of the Lord is on me, because he has anointed me to preach good news to the poor.*

"Preaching outside makes my skin crawl," he admitted to himself that night. Yet the next morning he awoke singing a hymn.

Sunday he found himself following Whitefield's very footsteps of the previous Sunday. Would anyone show up for the unknown John Wesley? In Bristol he preached at seven in the morning. Praise the Lord—about one thousand showed up. Then he preached at Hannam Mount in Kingswood to about fifteen hundred, he guessed, then continued to the other side of Kingswood and Rose Green. There in the afternoon he preached to five thousand!

At the end of the day he realized he had preached to seventy-five hundred people. "How many pulpits would it take to reach that many? And these dear people stand outside in the elements!"

Who could contest this field preaching? Who could question that it executed the Great Commission? And who, in a moment's reflection, could not remember that the Sermon on the Mount was field preaching?

Still, John did not feel comfortable. But why should he seek comfort? He had never admitted to doing that. He had rejected the soft life long ago. He wanted to bear a cross. If this kind of preaching made him uncomfortable, praise the Lord! So much the better.

A few days later, he was preaching inside to a society. He was such a draw now and the room was so packed the floor collapsed! Perhaps he would have to preach outside just to prevent such destruction.

By early May, John had made such a commitment to preaching in the Bristol area and he had such a following in the societies at Nicholas and Baldwin streets he was able to use their donations and his own money to buy a lot in the Horse Fair near Saint James's churchyard. Things were happening so fast the first stone was laid three days later. "And I have incurred a personal debt of one hundred and fifty pounds!" he told his friends, not in complaint but wonder. "But we must have a place to gather. We must do more than preach. We must follow through."

Yes, wonders seemed to come every day now. The world was turning upside down. George Whitefield now had brother Charles field preaching in the environs of London. John had Bristol to himself. He had worried he gradually would lose Whitefield's following. But instead, he built on it. One Sunday in early June, John preached to six thousand at Hannam Mount, then eight thousand at Rose Green, then to several hundred in their new building at the Horse Fair in Bristol. The sermon there was preached in a long room. He spoke from a desk facing the congregation, who sat on benches. Two sconces, each with eight candles, lit the room. Off to the side of the long room was a smaller room, intended for school and small meetings. John slept in a garret under the ceiling. A stable in back sheltered horses. He didn't dare think of this building as a church. Splitting off from the Church of England was unthinkable. If people had to have a name, let them call it the "New Room" for the "Methodist Society," John said. These small societies were called "Methodists" by outsiders anyway. There was nothing John could do to stop it.

"The name 'Methodist' sticks to me like a burr," he muttered.

John's preaching was not the only magnet to his sermons. Two other things drew the curious: hymns and hysteria. The Church of England only chanted psalms lifelessly. Both Wesleys long had thought that was a deficiency. The Bible advocated praise in the form of singing. And the English people loved to sing.

The Wesleys now regularly lead spirited hymns. The poetic Charles began to write his own hymns. John's message was hard, but oh—the joy of those hymns!

Hysteria was never seen in the church of England. From the very beginning of his outdoor preaching, people groaned, screamed and swooned. He was astonished. At one very early meeting, a Quaker was visibly appalled to hear the cacophony of groans and cheers. Suddenly, in mid-protest, he himself fell and rolled in agony before rising to his knees and crying, "Now I know thou art a prophet of the Lord!"

"How far I've departed from the sedate ritual of the Church of England!" John marveled.

John was next drawn to Bath, a mere stroll of hours from Bristol. But there were no grimy miners there. Bath was known for its waters. And the rich gathered to bathe and frolic. Bath was dominated by a dandy named Beau Nash.

John began to preach there, as usual by lambasting the crowd in his reasoned voice as all sinners, "high and low, rich and poor, one with another."

Suddenly an elegant golden carriage pulled by six white horses thundered to the edge of the crowd. Hanging on the outside of the carriage were outriders and footmen, even lackeys blowing French horns! Leaving the carriage and swaggering through the crowd was Beau Nash himself: silken, satined, ruffled, bejeweled, elegant.

"By what authority do you preach, sir?" he asked imperiously.

"By the authority of Jesus Christ, conveyed to me by the Archbishop of Canterbury, when he laid hands upon me and said, 'Take thou authority to preach the Gospel.' "

Nash snorted. "This meeting outside the church is illegal."

"Only seditious meetings are illegal."

"Then I say this one is seditious. You scare people out of their wits."

An old woman exploded, "You take care of your body, Mr. Nash. We will take care of our own souls, thank you. That's why we've come here."

Chastised by a commoner, Nash walked away in disgust. John went on preaching.

John's prison work had prepared him well to talk directly to the common people. And they seemed very eager to listen to him—eager enough to stand up to Nash. The dandy sensed John's drawing power.

A few days later, John joined Charles and Whitefield south of London at Blackheath. Whitefield surprised John by asking him to preach to the thousands gathered there in the open heathlands.

In the days ahead, there were crowds enough for all three in the great open areas around London. Highwaymen terrorized these lonely spaces at night, and the new field preachers proclaimed the Gospel to thousands by day. They spoke at Moorfields in north London and at Kennington Common east of London.

A peculiar thing was noted. Although Whitefield spoke with much more emotion than John, he would not allow any demonstrations of hysteria. Such a person promptly was escorted away. On the other hand, John, who spoke so calmly, allowed the demonstration to run its course, believing it to be a manifestation of the work of God. Charles, who spoke more emotionally than John but not as emotionally as Whitefield, was appalled by these outbursts. "I'll not allow such violent demonstrations," Charles insisted, and he suppressed them as Whitefield did.

After Whitefield sailed for America, John realized the irony. All of England was ripe for the Word, yet the most dynamic preacher in England was gone. John must fill the breach. He began to preach in more places now, even venturing into Wales. The crowds grew in the hinterlands. Ten thousand. Fifteen thousand. Twenty thousand. Most were no more than curious at first about this "Methodist" and his hymns and the hysteria he induced. But it brought them to the Gospel. They heard his hard message. They had to make a choice.

Spreading the Gospel far and wide, yet establishing local societies, required the most methodical planning. John Wesley was just the man to do it. Because everyone called him "Methodist," he now had to explain the term himself, emphasizing that "Methodism" was not new at all, but true, old-time Christianity and true Church of England Christianity.

In order to evangelize more widely, he needed someone reliable to hold down the Bristol ministry. "Charles," he said to his favorite recruit, "I need your help."

"Let us hope it turns out better for me than America did," Charles muttered, not thinking to resist.

Living the faith was not just preaching to huge throngs. In October 1739, John was brought to the bedside of a young woman in Kingswood. Before he ever saw her he heard her screaming. Three men were holding her down. She was writhing. Her face contorted into anguish, then horror, then despair. Yet her eyes were dry as stone.

John winced. "The dogs of hell are gnawing on her heart."

She screamed, "I am damned. I am the devil's now. His I am. Him I must serve. With him I must go to hell. I will serve him. I cannot be saved. I must, I will be damned!" And she began praying to the devil.

John said loudly, "Arm of the Lord, awake, awake!" He was joined by the others.

As long as they implored the Lord, the woman was silent. But as soon as they stopped, she began screaming again. Then another woman was seized and began screaming that she, too, was damned.

John sent for Charles. It was many hours before the two women were calmed. When the Wesleys left the house, the two women were singing praise to God, who "stilled the enemy and the avenger."

Four days later, John was called back. One of the women was possessed again. She screamed in a deep voice, "No power, no power; no faith, no faith. She is mine. Her soul is mine. I have her and I will not let her go." This time John could not calm her.

One of the men in the house said, "I fear a demon speaks inside her now."

117

John barked at the woman, "Demon, I command you in the name of the Lord to tell me if you have a commission to torment any other souls hereabouts."

The woman snarled the names of two local women who were close friends. A man said, "The demon lies. They are in perfect health."

The household prayed for hours. Finally, the woman sat up, composed and cheerful. "Praise God, from whom all blessings flow," she said in her own voice.

But the ordeal was not over. The very next day, John stopped at the home of one of the two women named by the demon. Both young women who had been named were there. Before John's very eyes, both were seized. Restrained, they ranted and raved through the entire night before they were eventually calmed by continual prayers.

From his mother, John learned Brother Sammy had become very alarmed at what he and Charles were doing. Sammy wrote Susanna:

> . . . .*I heard you [were one of John's congregation]. Is it not enough that I am bereft of both my brothers, but must my mother follow too? . . .They design separation. They are already forbidden all the pulpits in London; and. . .in all likelihood, it will come to the same all over England, if the bishops have courage enough. . . .I am not afraid the Church should excommunicate [John and Charles], but that [John and Charles] should excommunicate the Church!*

"How dare he make such a harsh judgment," John said. But he felt no anger, only sadness. He would talk to Sammy.

Sammy was a good-hearted, reasonable man.

But just three weeks later, John learned there would be no reconciliation with Sammy. . . .

ten

Foundations

Brother Sammy suddenly died in Tiverton. It was crushing to John. Now he could not reconcile himself with Sammy. He was even too late for the funeral. He stood over the grave in the cold November air, grieving a death so sudden.

Sammy had gotten sick in the night. By seven in the morning he was dead. The brothers and sisters owed Sammy so much. He was like a second father.

"And he died feeling betrayed and humiliated by his brothers," John admitted. "Following Christ exacts a heavy toll."

John had to carry his grief with him. He had too much to do. They needed a base in London. North of the Thames, in the sprawling area called Moorfields, John bought a foundry for 115 pounds. The large building with a few enormous rooms was once the Royal Arsenal. Many hundred pounds would be needed to renovate it. But it would see hard use, when finished. The chapel was to be galleried and hold up to seventeen hundred people. An adjoining chamber that would hold up to three hundred would be a school room. Above the school room were living quarters. Soon, mother Susanna was living there, then sister Emily, whose husband had died.

The "Foundry" offered prayer services at five o'clock in the morning and nine o'clock at night. John did not always conduct the services. His field preaching had not abated.

Nevertheless, he was able to start a work program at the Foundry. "Twelve of the poorest of the poor are given work each day carding and spinning cotton," he told Charles.

John's schedule was nonstop activity every waking moment, whether it was preaching to thousands or alone in prayer. He broke with the Fetter Lane society, which now was dominated by Moravians. James Hutton had even joined their church. As much as John admired the Moravians, he could not accept their "quietism," the notion that one must do nothing until some form of guidance is received from God.

John now had little tolerance for mystical elements. Upon reading William Law's latest book, he noted, "Philosophical, speculative, precarious, behemish, void, and vain!"

In going through all his old correspondence at Oxford, where he still held a room, he noted in his journal, "Should I conceal a sad truth, or declare it for the profit of others?" Then he revealed his belief that the only correspondent to show a true inner religion was regarded as a madman who, despised and forsaken, had died in youth. He was William Morgan.

Death struck the Wesleys again in March 1741. Kezzy died, almost on her thirty-second birthday. It was not unexpected, and Charles was with her. She had been especially close to Charles, as Patty was close to John. John fought the ugly resentment that gnawed at him—that Kezzy had never been healthy since Westley Hall had jilted her. Once a tight, disciplined family of a dozen under the rule of Samuel and Susanna, the Wesleys had scattered across England, and four already had fallen.

It was amid this grief and simmering anger against Westley Hall that John learned George Whitefield, back in England, was preaching against the Wesley brothers! This shocked John. He always had considered Whitefield to be part of the ministry with Charles and himself. And because Whitefield was still only twenty-seven, whereas John was thirty-eight, John considered the younger man his protégé. John rushed to see him.

"Yes, it's true," Whitefield admitted. "You and Charles preach a different Gospel from mine."

"But we differ only on predestination, a theological point," John said calmly. "You know how I feel on theology. Methodists can embrace different opinions. It is only conduct that excludes some from the Methodists. I would gladly welcome a Quaker into our company."

"I think, Brother, you feel stronger than that about predestination."

"Predestination is one of the foundation stones of the Church of England. Article Seventeen. We both agree on that."

"That is true. But you've embraced a far simpler thing than Article Seventeen. You speak of simple predestination. You've been deceived by that mongrel Arminianism. I speak of the pure form, truer to the nature of God, the real essence of Article Seventeen."

"Charles and I refuse to believe that people are predestined to be saved or damned. We cannot believe men have no free will to escape sin and find salvation. . . ."

Whitefield folded his hands. "Yes, I've read your fiery sermon on 'Free Grace.' That sermon does not make predestination sound like a minor theological point."

"I didn't say 'minor,' friend." John tried to keep the heat out of his voice, but he couldn't. "Your form of predestination represents God as worse than the devil!"

"You see. It is a real sticking point."

"I thought we resolved long ago to remain silent on our theological differences. When the Fetter Lane society became too

123

mystical for us, Charles and I quietly withdrew."

"I changed my mind. Our paths cross too often. People are confused. It's time we agree to disagree—publicly."

"I believe you have been corrupted by the great Calvinist, Mr. Edwards, of New England," John said bluntly. "And I also believe you now differ with the Church of England."

John had not wanted to mention Edwards. It sounded like he was jealous. Edwards and Whitefield had set New England ablaze with their preaching in 1740. Some in America called it the "Great Awakening."

Whitefield replied, "I, sir, believe you are the one who differs from the Church of England. You've moved beyond our Methodism."

Both seemed to calm as they reflected on their accusations. They were both very averse to appearing to split from the Church of England. That was the hammer their critics used on them. Both John and Whitefield insisted Methodists were a society of Anglicans seeking holiness. They had no intention of forming a new church. John was glad they parted with a handshake.

The two remained friends, just as John and Peter Boehler remained friends in spite of John's dislike of the Moravians' quietism. But the confusing issue of predestination remained a stumbling block. It was no small issue with John. The sum of Calvin's predestination is this, John thought: "Certain people are selected before they are ever born to be saved, and they will be saved at the end of their earthly life, do what they will. Likewise, certain people are damned before they are ever born and they will be damned, do what they will.

"I will never believe that! What would I do if I thought the Church of England really did advocate Calvin's cruel brand of predestination?"

Another crisis arose. John had several laymen in his

societies he trusted to give advice to those people who needed it, to pray with those who asked and even to expound on
the Bible, if needed. Ever since John Bray had astounded
John in the Fetter Lane society, John had known some lay
people carried the Bible in their hearts. Such people knew
the Gospel as well as a cleric from Oxford.

One such man was Thomas Maxfield, whom John had
recruited in Bristol, then sent to London. But John heard a
rumor that Maxfield had crossed the line, and he rushed to
London.

"Lies are circulating that Maxfield is preaching," he told
his mother. "I'm here to put that falsehood to rest."

"He is preaching," Susanna replied. "And he preaches
quite well."

"This is highly irregular!" John complained.

"Yes, it is," she agreed. She added softly, "John, I'm the
daughter of an Oxford graduate, ordained as minister so he
could preach. I'm the wife of an Oxford graduate, ordained
as minister so he could preach. I'm the mother of three
Oxford graduates, ordained as ministers so they could
preach. I've heard Thomas Maxfield preach. He is as surely
called by God to preach as any of you are."

So John, the stickler for liturgical details, did not dismiss
Maxfield on the spot. He listened to him preach. In the back
of his mind was the hope that his mother was wrong.
Perhaps Maxfield was not really preaching. Perhaps he was
merely expounding on the Bible, as they so often did in their
small society meetings. But no. Maxfield was really preaching. And his sermon was letter-perfect. It could have been
written by John himself.

What could John say? When he saw his mother again, he
confided, "It is of God." And from that day on, lay preachers were part of the Methodist societies. But it was another

duty for John, for he must approve the fitness of each and every one. And they needed a set of definite rules.

Soon, any Methodist who had dreams of being a lay preacher knew John's stringent requirements:

1. *Be diligent. Never be unemployed a minute. . . .*
2. *Be serious. . . .Avoid all lightness, jesting. . . .*
3. *Converse sparingly. . .with women, particularly with young women.*
4. *Take no step toward marriage, without first consulting with your brethren.*
5. *Believe evil of no one. . . .*
6. *Speak evil of no one. . . .*
7. *Tell everyone what you think wrong in him. . . .*
8. *Do not [act]. . .the gentleman. . . .*
9. *Be ashamed of nothing but sin: not of fetching wood . . . or drawing water. . . .*
10. *Be punctual. Do everything exactly on time. . . .*
11. *It is not your business to preach so many times, and to take care of this or that society, but to save as many souls as you can. . . .*
12. *Act in all things, not according to your own will, but as a son in the Gospel. . . .*

If a prospective preacher's green ambition could weather those twelve searing rules, John added the burden of "unofficial" rules. The preacher should spend five hours a day reading. The preaching itself was to "1. invite, 2. convince, 3. offer Christ, and 4. build up." Any preacher of John's was organized every waking minute.

John now often faced much more immediate danger than organizational or theological difficulties. His growing popularity had brought murderous opposition to the surface.

Perhaps it wasn't intended to be so drastic, but who could tell what a mob would do when goaded and riled? Often, now, he faced paid rabble. In July 1741, at Charles Square in London—a favorite pulpit for the Methodists—a gang ran an ox into the crowd. The miscreants tried to direct it to trample someone, but they could not control the animal. Finally, the enormous beast broke away and disappeared down the road.

John realized later he'd had no fear whatever in the encounter. Did it mean he finally had total trust in God, like the youngest Moravians had? Or had his methodical mind rationalized the ox was frightened and the gang incompetent?

Late in 1741, John was stricken with fever in Bristol. Sammy had succumbed quickly to fever, as many had. So any fever was frightening.

John's fever was severe. It was the worst illness he had ever had. He was bed-ridden. His fever peaked and died, but when he worked again, the fever flared up to peak again, then died again. He had a peculiar disease, perhaps a remnant of some infection from America. Physicians had seen this cycling of fever in those who had traveled in hot, moist climates.

In early 1742, John was tested again by a mob, this time in London at a house on Long Lane. A gang broke into the meeting and started tearing up the house. Outside, they were hurling large stones onto the roof. The congregation inside was being battered by falling tiles and stones. John finally asked several men in the congregation to go outside and seize one man. "That is the man we shall take to the constable," John shouted.

The men seized one of mob and dragged him inside. The crowd outside chanted his name. He was one of the ringleaders. Yes, the mob wanted more trouble. Yet when the man stood inside, facing John, he suddenly fell to his knees, apparently struck down by remorse. An abusive woman who forced her way in with him was struck down, as well, screaming praise for God's mercy. The tense situation evaporated.

On March 10, 1742, near Pensford a gang of men scattered the crowd with a bull they had been baiting earlier with dogs. They drove the poor beast into the table John was standing on. The bull was very tired, and John simply pushed its head aside to keep the blood off his cassock. John's supporters rescued him and carried him away on their shoulders. He looked back to see the table disintegrate. Again, he had no fear whatever. But the doubt remained as to whether he had true trust in God or merely the composure to quickly assess the poor beast was exhausted.

On May 27, 1742, he arrived in Newcastle, the great coal town in the north. It was not his first trip there, but never before had the town seemed so decadent. The town appealed to him immediately for all the "wrong" reasons.

"So much drunkenness, cursing and swearing—even from the mouths of children—I have never witnessed before in such a short time," he told his companions. "Surely this place is ripe for Him who 'came not to call the righteous, but sinners to repentance.' "

"But they may not answer the call," replied John Taylor, one of his companions.

At seven o'clock Sunday morning, John preached on a hillside in Sandgate, the poorest slum of the town. It appeared no one was going to answer the call, but three or four drifted out of their shacks to gawk at his vestments. The number grew to a few hundred, then to one thousand. After his sermon, they were glum, silent. Were they entranced or just dull?

"My name is John Wesley," he said. "At five in the evening, with God's help, I intend to preach here on this very spot again."

That evening when he returned, he could scarcely believe his eyes. The crowd was greater than his voice. It was the largest crowd he had ever seen. People blanketed the hill and beyond. His voice was strong, and he may have reached twenty-five or thirty thousand of them. He could not know. They almost trampled him afterward. They followed him to his inn, begging him to stay. They were starved for God's Word.

"Newcastle is truly meant to be the third base in our organization," he told his companions. "With it we will have a far-flung triangular base that will cover all of England: Bristol to London to Newcastle."

On the way back to London, John stopped in Epworth. He had not been to his hometown in many years. He advised the curate of Saint Andrew's, John Romley, he would gladly help with the sermon or prayers. Romley refused his help. And the curate's sermon pointedly warned against "enthusiasts."

Was John once again tangled in the past? Yes, Romley was hostile, but who in Epworth still remembered he had courted Hetty and had been turned away as a poor prospect? And who in Epworth still remembered he became curate only after all the Wesley sons refused to be its rector?

After the sermon, John Taylor stood outside the church as people were coming out. He shouted, "Mr. Wesley, not being permitted to preach in the church, intends to preach here at six o'clock."

At six o'clock, John stood on top of his father's tombstone to speak on a passage in Romans 14: *For the kingdom of God is not a matter of eating and drinking, but of righteousness, peace and joy in the Holy Spirit.* He had seen many congregations in his years at Epworth, but this was the largest ever. Even dead Mary's husband John Whitelamb was there; Whitelamb did not speak to John afterward, but slipped away. John soon heard rumors he had lost his faith.

The response in Epworth was so enthusiastic John stayed longer. He ignored John Romley's slights and politely deferred requests for baptisms and Holy Communion to the curate.

John visited Wroot. There Whitelamb was indeed in spiritual turmoil. Whitelamb felt remorse over interfering with Kezzy's life, and his poor Mary was buried in the churchyard. Was it any wonder he avoided John Wesley? Yet he was still curate there, and he stepped forward to offer John his church. So John preached at Wroot. The response there, too, was on a magnitude never seen before. John wrote joyously in his journal:

> *Oh let none think his labor of love is lost because the fruit does not immediately appear! Near forty years did my father labor here; but he saw little fruit of his labor. I took some pains among these people too; and my strength also seemed spent in vain; but now the fruit has appeared. There were scarce any in the town on whom either my father or I had taken any pains formerly but the seed, sown so long since, now sprung up, bringing forth repentance and remission of sins.*

He went on to Bristol. There he received news that made the sweet honey of his triumphant homecoming at Epworth turn to sand in his mouth: his mother was gravely ill.

When John reached his mother at his living quarters upstairs in the Foundry on July 18, 1742, he saw she was already on "the borders of eternity." He remembered only too well how his father had died, the professions of wanting to depart and be with Christ broken by the spells of gasping, fighting for life. Susanna was retracing Samuel's journey. John's sisters were there—even the elusive Anne. They watched their mother slowly sink. Five days later her soul departed.

John said, "Sisters, let us sing a psalm of praise to God, just as mother asked."

Susanna Wesley was seventy-two years old. She was buried nearby at Bunhill Fields, off City Road. She was in the company of distinguished Noncomformists; not only John Bunyan was buried there, but also Daniel Defoe, who had been a close friend of Samuel Wesley from his Oxford days.

A throng was there to pay their respects. It was one of the saddest moments of John's life delivering a eulogy developed from Revelation 20:

> *Then I saw a great white throne and him who was seated on it. Earth and sky fled from his presence, and there was no place for them. And I saw the dead, great and small, standing before the throne, and books were opened. Another book was opened, which is the book of life. The dead were judged according to what they had done as recorded in the books.*

John had not the slightest doubt how his mother would be judged.

After the funeral, the brothers and sisters reminisced. They were no longer children, to be sure. Emily was now fifty. Charles, the youngest, was thirty-four. They couldn't recall the last time they had been all together—perhaps nearly twenty years before, at Epworth. They seemed to be mourning for their fallen father, brother and sisters, too. But Mother Susanna was on their minds.

Patty started it. "I recall one of Mother's favorite expressions: 'Take care of the world, lest it unawares steals away your heart.' "

"And I recall," Charles added, "Mother saying, 'Do not live like the rest of mankind, who pass through the world like straws upon a river, which are carried whichever way the stream or wind drives them.' "

Anne brightened. "And she told me, 'Give God the praise for any well-spent day.' "

John smiled. "And she wisely warned me, 'Be very cautious in giving fine distinctions in public assemblies, for it does not answer the true end of preaching, which is to mend men's lives. . . .' "

"And she advised me," Hetty said, "to 'make poetry sometimes your diversion, though never your business.' "

Sukey added sadly, "My counsel was that the 'best preparation for suffering is a regular and exact performance of present duties.' "

Emily laughed with some bitterness. "And I recall her advice to 'be content to fill a little space if God be glorified.' "

"Well, each of us has spoken," John said. "It seems Mother is not gone at all. She rests in all our hearts, as pure as gold."

eleven

First Conference

John now devoted much time to Newcastle. He was anxious to build a "room" there, too, which was his modest way of describing a community center for worship and school. He acquired land outside the Pilgrim Street Gate in late 1742, laying the first stone the following January. What faith to plan a building that would cost seven hundred pounds when his total assets were twenty-six pounds!

In March, he preached on the parable of the Rich Man and Lazarus at its opening. The building would come to be known as Orphan House. It would house a chapel, a school, a book shop, living quarters for itinerant preachers, even a hospital—but never an orphanage.

Satisfied, he mounted his horse. "Now, back to London."

Just weeks later, on May 29, he started another center in London, this one on West Street. His appeal was so great that when he first preached in its chapel, there were many times the number that could be seated. So he preached on the third chapter of John for five hours to congregations admitted in relays. Then he went to Great-Gardens where he preached again, this time on the passage "You must be born again."

He was not welcome everywhere. His excursions into new regions of England were always dangerous. In Darlington, thirty miles from Newcastle, both his horse and his companion's horse began to stagger. The poor beasts laid down and died. Someone had poisoned them.

On another trip, he was in the west Midlands in the village of Wednesbury, writing at a friend's house after preaching. A mob gathered outside.

"Go outside and bring their ringleaders to me," John asked his hosts matter-of-factly.

His serenity seemed to always calm his foes, and it worked again. After the ringleaders were calmed, he went outside with them. The mob of several hundred screamed they wanted justice. John complied. They rushed off toward the magistrate in spite of pouring rain.

To the judge they cried, "This man makes people sing psalms all day and get up at five in the morning!"

"Go home," he muttered, and refused to talk more with them.

The mob rushed John off to another justice in Walsal. There, another mob met the first one. They scuffled for control of John. John tried to duck inside a house, but someone grabbed him by his hair and pulled him back into the crowd.

He yelled, "Are you willing to hear me speak?"

"Knock his brains out!" some yelled.

"Kill him!" others cried.

"Listen to him speak," shouted another.

After John was allowed to speak for about fifteen minutes, the competing mobs became impatient. Again they scuffled, and one mob rushed him back toward Wednesbury. He was hemmed in on all sides. There was no escape. Many were trying to knock him down. One man whacked at him with a club.

John remembered only too well other incidents in other towns. He always had been lucky enough to escape death. Once a brick grazed his shoulder. Once a stone struck him between the eyes. Once he got punched in the mouth. Already this night he'd had his clothes torn. His hand was scraped raw. His hair had been yanked. He had been punched hard twice. Blood was oozing from his mouth.

"Unhand him! Or you'll all be in the dungeon!"

It was the mayor of Wednesbury. He took John back to his friend's house. At last it was over. John was overjoyed. He had felt no pain at all. And fear had been utterly gone. He could have been sitting by the fireside during the ordeal, he was so composed. He truly felt in God's hands. He had passed the test at last. God had blessed him this night.

Just three days later he almost drowned. He was supposed to preach in Grimsby, not far from Epworth. But heavy rains had swollen the Trent. The ferrymen did not want to cross the river. John pestered them until they did. Halfway across, the barge capsized, with horses and men tumbling into the torrent. Yet the barge would not sink. The ferrymen were astounded and poled the barge to the other side. All were safe, even those who fell into the river.

Once the barge was tethered, John discovered he could not move. He seemed frozen to the bottom of the vessel. A large iron crowbar had slipped though a loop on his boot and a plank of the barge. If the barge had sunk, John would have gone down with it.

"Praise the Lord. Surely God kept the barge afloat," John said.

In Spring 1744, he felt compelled to write King George the Second. John's enemies had told the king John Wesley was sympathetic to the Jacobites, a group of people who opposed the current kings of the House of Hanover and wished to restore a king from the House of Stuart. The current candidate from the House of Stuart was the grandson of King James the Second. Charles Edward Stuart, a young man of just twenty-three, was called Bonnie Prince Charlie by those who supported him.

The charge that John was a supporter was absurd. Brother Sammy also had been accused of being a Jacobite. So had John's father. It stemmed from their friendship with Dean Atterbury, dead now but truly a Jacobite in his day. John would have shrugged off the slander, but Bonnie Prince Charlie was thought to be organizing an invasion from France. If war broke out, the first people locked up by King George naturally would be the known Jacobites.

In total sincerity, John wrote his "gracious sovereign":

> *We cannot, indeed, say or do either more or less than we apprehend consistent with the Word of God; but we are ready to obey your Majesty to the uttermost in all things we conceive to be agreeable thereto. And we earnestly exhort all with whom we converse, as they fear God, to honor the King. We of the clergy in particular put all men in mind to revere the higher powers as of God. . . .Silver and gold. . .we have none; but such as we have we humbly beg your Majesty to accept together with our hearts and prayers. . . .*

In summer 1744, the leaders of the Methodist societies held their first conference in London. Meeting were John, Charles, four others ordained as clergy of the Church of England, plus four lay preachers.

The ten leaders first discussed doctrine. What did they mean by justification? Repentance? Saving faith? Sanctification?

"Leaders of our societies shall not use pious phrases that they themselves cannot explain," John said. "And we must wherever possible use simple, everyday words."

He discouraged the use of the elaborate, expansive manner of speaking considered cultured among the gentry. The gentry embellished every statement; no gentleman said in three words what could be said in thirty.

"Pray, do not speak as the gentry do," John said. He demonstrated by tilting his nose up in the air and speaking, "Believe me, good sir, I have scarce words to express the exultation I feel upon your most fortuitous alliance with the esteemed and honorable Mr. Pepperwit." John lowered his nose. "But say this: 'I'm glad you know Mr. Pepperwit, sir.' "

Ever since John first had visited prisoners at Oxford, he had known that a florid, upper class manner of speaking not only tried the patience of commoners, but the meaning eluded most of them. John thought he had changed his speech to their liking, but once he began field preaching, he tested a sermon in front of a housemaid. He implored her to stop him every time he used a word she did not understand. He was appalled to find she rarely let him finish a sentence. Since his Oxford days, many overblown expressions of the educated upper class had crept back into his speech. After that, he consciously labored to explain the Gospel in the simple, terse words it had been written in by church fathers.

"We should constantly use the most common, little, easy words, just so long as they are pure and proper for the meaning," he urged his preachers.

Only the most experienced preacher should attempt a sermon of more than a half hour. In fact, it would be constructive if the entire service were only a half hour. John wanted a hymn before and after the sermon.

This was the basic Methodist service. They did not perform the sacraments of baptism and Holy Communion. Hymns were so important they published a hymn book, *Hymns and*

Sacred Poems, followed by two more: *Moral and Sacred Hymns* and *Hymns for Times of Trouble and Persecution.*

For the hymn books, John translated the very best hymns from French, German and Spanish into English. On the other hand, poetic Charles was now writing his own. They were for every occasion: Sunday worship, funerals, Holy Communion, Christmas, Easter, public thanksgiving, children. No subject that concerned the church eluded him. He already had written "Jesus, Lover of My Soul," "And Can It Be That I Should Gain?," "Christ the Lord Is Risen Today" and "Depth of Mercy." But to be included in the hymn book, even Charles' hymns had to approved by John, who looked for inconsistencies with their theology. "It won't do to sing hymns that contradict our sermons!" John clucked.

John was a severe critic, but he praised the hymns of Charles to others—methodically, of course. "I think no one else composes hymns in the English language so full of Scripture. As to his poetry, there is no doggerel, no botches, nothing implanted to patch up the rhyme. No emotion is too bloated or bombastic on the one hand, or too low or creeping on the other. He uses no empty church palaver, but only words that express exactly what he means. He uses over twenty varieties of meter. His vivacity, variety and lyrical power, at their best, are excellent poetry."

But hymns like "Jesus, Lover of My Soul" transcended analysis. One only had to hear the joy:

> *Jesus, Lover of my soul,*
> *Let me to Thy bosom fly,*
> *While the nearer waters roll,*
> *While the tempest still is high;*
> *Hide me, O my Savior, hide,*
> *Till the storm of life is past;*

Safe into the haven guide,
O receive my soul at last.

Other refuge have I none,
Hangs my helpless soul on Thee;
Leave, ah, leave me not alone,
Still support and comfort me.
All my trust on Thee is stayed,
All my help from Thee I bring;
Cover my defenseless head
With the shadow of Thy wing.

Thou, O Christ, art all I want;
More than all in Thee I find;
Raise the fallen, cheer the faint,
Heal the sick and lead the blind.
Just and holy is Thy name,
I am all unrighteousness;
Vile and full of sin I am,
Thou art full of truth and grace.

Plenteous grace with Thee is found,
Grace to cover all my sin;
Let the healing streams abound;
Make and keep me pure within.
Thou of life the fountain art,
Freely let me take of Thee;
Spring Thou up within my heart,
Rise to all eternity.

"And Can It Be That I Should Gain?" seemed to condense John's own conversion in iambic octameter:

And can it be that I should gain
An interest in the Saviour's blood?
Died He for me, who caused His pain?
For me, who Him to death pursued?
Amazing love! How can it be;
That Thou my God, shouldst die for me?

He left His Father's throne above,
So free, so infinite His grace;
Emptied Himself of all but love,
And bled for Adam's helpless race;
'Tis mercy all, immense and free;
For, O my God, it found out me.

Long my imprisoned spirit lay,
Fast bound in sin and nature's night;
Thine eye diffused a quickening ray,
I woke, the dungeon flamed with light;
My chains fell off, my heart was free;
I rose, went forth, and followed Thee.

The ten conferees discussed the sacraments. Methodists would not perform sacraments, insisted both John and Charles. They would urge their members to attend their parish church to obtain the sacraments. In fact, no society meetings were ever to take place in the hour a local parish church was holding services. This conflict could not be tolerated.

Sacraments were not such a problem as some educated people believed, because so many people in the societies had never attended parish churches at all. They were truly the unchurched, discovering the Gospel because of the Methodists.

"Now, gentlemen," John said to the conferees, "we've

arrived at the heart of the societies: our membership. Has each member lived the Gospel?"

John was very tolerant on theological differences; that was why he was so surprised by Whitefield's public opposition. After all, weren't they all "fleeing the wrath of God," seeking holiness and perfection? But that tolerance did not stretch to conduct. Any member who did not conduct himself according to the Gospel had to depart. And living the Gospel had been set down by the Methodists as "General Rules."

"First, let us review our General Rules, brothers," John said. "Charles will read them."

The others listened as Charles read,

> *"There is only one condition previously required in those who desire admission into these societies, a desire 'to flee from the coming wrath' and to be saved from their sins. But wherever this is really fixed in the soul, it will be shown by its fruits. It is therefore expected of all who continue therein, that they should continue to evidence their desire of salvation.*
>
> *"First, by doing no harm; by avoiding evil in every kind; especially that which is most generally practiced. Such as:*
> *The taking of the name of God in vain;*
> *The profaning the day of the Lord, either by doing ordinary work thereon, or by buying or selling;*
> *Drunkenness, buying or selling spiritous liquors, or drinking them (unless in cases of extreme necessity);*
> *Fighting, quarreling, brawling; going to*

law, returning evil for evil or railing for
railing; the using many words in buying
or selling;

The buying or selling uncustomed [smug-
gled] goods;

The giving or taking things on usury;

Uncharitable or unprofitable conversation;

Doing to others as we would not they
should do unto us;

Doing what we know is not for the glory of
God: as

The putting on of gold, or costly apparel;

The taking of such diversions as cannot be
used in the name of the Lord Jesus;

The singing those songs, or reading those
books, which do not tend to the knowledge or love of God;

Softness, and needless self-indulgence;

Laying up treasures on earth.

It is expected of all who continue in these
societies that they should continue to
evidence their desire of salvation.

Secondly, by doing good; by being in every
kind, merciful after their power; as they
have opportunity, doing good of every
possible sort, and as far as possible, to
all men.

To their bodies, of the ability which God
giveth, by giving food to the hungry, by
clothing the naked, by visiting or helping them that are sick, or in prison:

To their souls, by instructing, reproving, or
exhorting all we have any intercourse

with; trampling underfoot that enthusi-
astic doctrine of devils, that 'we are not
to do good unless our heart is free to it.'
By doing good, especially, to them that are
of the household of faith, or groaning so
to be; employing them preferably to
others, buying one of another, helping
each other in business; and that so
much the more because the world will
love its own, and them only.
By all possible diligence and frugality, that
the Gospel be not blamed.
By running with patience the race that is set
before them; denying themselves and
taking up their cross daily; submitting
to bear the reproach of Christ, to be as
the filth and offscouring of the world;
and that men should say all manner of
evil of them falsely, for their Lord's
sake.
It is expected of all who continue in these
societies that they should continue to
evidence their desire of salvation.
Thirdly, by attending upon all the ordi-
nances of God, such are:
The public worship of God; the ministry of
the word, either read or expounded;
The supper of the Lord;
Private prayer;
Searching the Scriptures; and fasting, or
abstinence."

Charles took a deep breath and looked around at his

143

listeners. John spoke. "And which of our members fail our General Rules, not for human weakness but for lack of trying and bad faith, though admonished?"

The ten leaders went through their entire membership, commenting on every member. Eventually they reduced the total membership to nineteen hundred. Some of the leaders grew alarmed. One sighed, "We've cut so many."

"Numbers are not significant," John said. "May God increase our societies in faith and love."

They then discussed the garb of their preachers. Regardless of background, they must dress like gentlemen, to the best of their resources. Yet they must never sport silks or satins as dandies did. Colors of the long frock coats and knee pants were cool blues and grays. White shirts and stockings were expected to be clean. The headware was a three-cornered hat. Maintaining this crisp appearance after riding through squalling weather and grasping mobs was a challenge.

They discussed their "circuits." These were a network of societies each leader shepherded. And there was no way to do that except by riding a horse over the rough roads of England hours each day. John urged them to use this time to read, if it was not raining or sleeting. A man could read even astride a horse at a steady, brisk pace of about five miles an hour—not a trot, of course, which exhausted a rider after an hour or two, but a fast walk.

"Or you may write hymns while riding," John added as he eyed Charles, who composed hymns on horseback. Sometimes Charles exhausted his supplies and would dismount at his destination, yelling breathlessly, "Quick! Bring me pen and ink!"

At another level for the Methodists was the maintenance of local societies like those at London or Bristol that were growing into hundreds of followers. Here the Methodists had added a level called a class meeting. This was a group of twelve. The group discussed and resolved money requirements of the whole society, but its main function was accountability in the pursuit of holiness. This added facet of the Methodists was really based on the concept of the Holy Club and the Wesleys' first small societies. John realized this close-knit feeling of the small group must never be lost as the local societies grew larger and larger.

The class of twelve met once a week in the society building and sat around a table. On the table was a Bible, God's Word and their source of wisdom. Whoever the group had chosen as leader would blow on a pitchpipe and they would sing a hymn. They then would pray for the Holy Spirit to expose their thoughts and inspire them to holiness. After a Bible reading, the revelations began.

The leader would say, "Sister Smith, how has this past week been for your soul?"

Sister Smith would flush. "Praise the Lord, well, sir."

"Any temptations?" he would prod.

"Yes. God forgive me."

"Any more incidents of temper?"

"Yes. But fewer than before! And the week has brought many blessings to me."

"Go on to victory, Sister Smith. One day the crown incorruptible will be yours. Hallelujah. Brother Jones, how was the past week for your soul?"

And so they would proceed around the table. These public confessions in the class meeting made each member seek holiness with ardor. While each one answered the leader, the others were chanting concern or praise.

Every three months a "ticket" to the meetings was issued to members in good standing. After all, attending such a soul-baring meeting was a great privilege. A ticket was lost for three consecutive absences.

Eventually, one of the ten leaders at the Methodist conference in 1744 broached a very explosive subject. "Will we Methodists eventually separate from the Church of England? Aren't we even now challenging the authority of the bishops?"

"Certainly not, sir!" John answered.

"But in the event we are no longer able to lead, perhaps even at home with Christ, what might our membership do?" questioned the man softly.

John replied forcefully, "Even after our deaths, our Methodists will remain in the Church of England, unless the church throws them out!" But as he studied their faces, he saw that even Charles looked skeptical.

They agreed such a conference should be held every year, and returned to their circuits. John promised to put more advice in writing. Even traveling four thousand miles a year now, it was getting harder and harder for him to visit every society. He would issue rules of conduct. He would issue guidelines for preaching. His duties seemed boundless.

John returned to Oxford in August to preach at Saint Mary's. He was quite a curiosity now, this firebrand who claimed to be an instrument of the Church of England but appeared to be creating something new. The congregation was hushed, on the edge of their seats. Was John a hypocrite or a crackpot? Would he dare lambaste this distinguished gathering like he did the commoners?

twelve

Growth

*T*he John Wesley who faced the Oxford elite was a man of forty-one, scarred by mobs. The sheltered, pampered nature in these Oxford men inflamed him. The towering church spire that dominated the skyline seemed a lightning rod, from which he drew fiery energy.

Two-thirds of his sermon was unexceptional. It was a description of the activity and influence of the Holy Spirit in the early church. It was a nice, reasoned history that comforted the Oxfordians. But their comfort soon ended.

John declared England not a Christian country.

He declared Oxford not a Christian city.

The students were triflers.

The fellows of the colleges had Holy Orders, but they were slackers.

The heads of the colleges were not of one heart and one soul in the Holy Spirit.

After the sermon, the vice-chancellor demanded a copy of John's sermon. Charles paled. "This is the first step of a rigid procedure that bans a preacher from speaking at Oxford."

John was very pleased, though. "Wonderful. Now every man of eminence in the university will read the stinging barbs in my sermon, which might have otherwise died by neglect. And they will never ask me to speak again. I'm free of the blood of these men."

But Oxford chose to let the matter drop. Banning John would only create more curiosity.

John continued riding far and near to visit his societies and start new ones. But by July 1745, the English people were less and less tolerant to itinerant travelers. All strangers were suspected of being spies. The reason was that Bonnie Prince Charlie had landed in Scotland and gathered a force of highlanders around him.

John and the Methodists were badgered everywhere. His young preachers were grabbed and thrown into military service. It was a bad time to be doing anything different. In Gwennap, he was roughly seized himself for military duty, but within minutes he was released, having soothed his captor. At Falmouth a mob stormed the house John was in.

A woman of the house cried, "Hide yourself in the closet." "No," John answered. "It is best I stand just as I am."

At that moment the front door ripped off the hinges and came crashing down. John immediately pushed his way into the mob before they could enter the house.

"Well, here I am," he said calmly but very loudly in his practiced voice. "To which of you have I done any wrong?" He looked about him. "You? Or you? Or you?" The crowd was silent. So John began a sermon, and they listened without interrupting.

Later he marveled. Surely the hand of God protected him that day. He had not seen one man in Falmouth who could have come to his aid. Yet unlike the mob at Wednesbury, not one man here had so much as lifted an arm against him. The one similarity between the two incidents was John's total lack of fear.

Time and time again John faced such incidents. Once he was pushed off a wall as he spoke—the prelude to violence. Yet he grabbed the hand of an attacker who had seemed mildly sympathetic and reasoned with his adversaries. Soon the man was defending him, and the tension evaporated.

He returned to Bristol August 1 for the second annual conference with as "many of the brethren that labor in the Word as could be present." After several days he headed north. In Leeds he was pelted with dirt and stones. In Newcastle he ran headlong into the "rebellion." Bonnie Prince Charlie had just captured Edinburgh with his highlanders. The gates to Newcastle were being walled up, including Pilgrims Gate. The Methodists' so-called Orphan House was now outside the city walls!

Soon they heard the news that the highlanders of Bonnie Prince Charlie had fought Gen. Cope's British force at Prestonpans, outside Edinburg, and defeated them in ten minutes! There was no force now to stop the Jacobite rebels from pushing south one hundred miles to the nearest prize: Newcastle! In his journal, John recorded for September 22:

> *The walls are mounted with cannon, and all things prepared for sustaining an assault. Meantime our poor neighbors, on either hand, were busy removing their goods. And most of the best houses in our street were left without either furniture or inhabitants. Those within the walls were almost equally busy in carrying away their money and goods; and more and more of the gentry every hour rode southward as fast as they could. At eight I preached at Gateshead. . . . How do all things tend to the furtherance of the Gospel! All this week the alarms from the north continued, and the storm seemed nearer every day. Many wondered (if we Methodists would stay outside) the walls. Others told us we must remove quickly; for if the cannon began to play from the top of the gates, they would beat all the house*

[down] about our ears. . . .

But John did not abandon his Orphan House. He continued to preach, finding ready audiences seeking comfort. The region around Newcastle was under great tension. Even the country gentlemen had abandoned their estates to hide inside the city walls of Newcastle.

But in November, John learned the rebels had crossed the Tweed River and raced south. They had bypassed the northern cities, including Newcastle!

John's time at Newcastle had not been all stressful. He rediscovered the very attractive Grace Murray. John had transferred her there from his center in London because she was a native of Newcastle. But he only now realized how unusually competent she was. She was the leader of several classes of twelve. Temperamentally, she was like his favorite sister Patty. She was cheerful and never complained.

The Methodist center at this time required much attention to housing itinerant preachers, to schooling poor children and to providing medical care. Always blunt, John abruptly told Grace Murray, "I now realize that no one is better qualified than you to run those operations."

Leaving Orphan House in Grace's charge, long-delayed from his own travel plans, John rode south. Everywhere he was stopped by watchmen. The towns were lit by bonfires at night. Everyone expected to be attacked by the rebels.

Bonnie Prince Charlie and his Scottish army soon came into the north country again, their advance thwarted at Derby in the Midlands. They retreated to Scotland. In April 1746 at Culloden Moor, sixteen thousand men battled. Bonnie Prince Charlie and his highlanders were defeated. The rebellion ended. The perpetrator escaped to France, free to plot again. More than a thousand of his officers and gentlemen remained behind to be executed.

The rebellion over, John embarked on a much more mundane venture. After visiting Bristol, he decided in London to end his slavery to tea. The battle was undertaken to show others it could be done. The motive was to inspire the poor to spend no money on such a worthless item as tea.

The battle with tea was far from easy. John had drunk tea several times a day for twenty-six years. For three days he had a dull headache and felt tired every waking minute. The third afternoon he lost his memory. His memory crept back that evening. He prayed and prayed that night. The next day he felt as fit as ever. Tea was beaten. "The severe effects of its denial only prove how corrupting it was," John said, memory fully restored.

The surrender of tea was an outgrowth of John's concern with health and the treatment of illnesses. In London he had opened a dispensary, employing a pharmacist and a physician. He even worked there himself, being widely read on medicines. Once in America he had even assisted a physician in an autopsy. He was very confident in his ability to diagnose and had given medical treatment often in his preaching journeys; if the patient betrayed a lack of faith in John, he always tried to get a regular physician. Naturally, John was criticized. So he wrote in his journal:

> . . . .*Ought I to have let one of these poor wretches perish, because I was not a regular physician?*

Not satisfied with that local effort in London, John was writing a book called *An Easy and Natural Method of Curing Most Diseases.* In it he would prescribe 725 prescriptions for 243 diseases. His prescriptions were usually very simple ones people could obtain easily. He did not believe in complicated compounds "consisting of so many ingredients that is scarce possible for common people to know which it was that wrought the cure." He fully intended to distribute this book to every member of the societies.

"Servants for God need to stay healthy," he insisted.

John certainly needed his own good health, because he had a relentless schedule that required him to travel more than four thousand miles a year. He visited his societies, held together by his triangle of centers at London, Newcastle and Bristol. Nothing stopped him.

February 16, 1747, he and his companions rose at three in the morning to journey north from London, noting the unseasonably mild weather. It soon changed, a north wind blowing snow into their faces. That was only a prelude. Soon hail was blasting them so hard they could not see and could scarcely breathe. They hunkered down and prayed the horses could stay on the roadway. Yet at six that night John preached in Potten, nearly forty miles north of London.

The next morning, they had a different problem. The untracked snow was a brilliant white canvas with nothing marking the road. The horses were stumbling. Soon that problem seemed trivial: they were pelted by sleet, which froze instantly to whatever it struck. They stopped at shelter whenever they could to break out of their encasing ice, then pushed on. At sunset, they reached an inn at Brigcasterton, nearly thirty miles from Potten!

The next morning, one of John's helpers said, "Sir, they tell me there is no traveling today. The horses cannot follow the road. It is impassable."

"We'll lead them, then," John said.

And the Methodists set out on foot to face a fierce northeast wind. They threaded their way through huge dunes of snow, leading their horses. They had to leave the road time and time again because enormous drifts blocked their way. By evening they reached Newark-on-the-Trent, twenty miles north of Brigcasterton. John had a toothache so painful he could not speak.

He was no less determined by river or sea. He tolerated few excuses for not pushing ahead. Once at Holyhead, a port favored for sailing to Ireland, he uncharacteristically fumed to his companions, "I never knew men could make such poor, lame excuses as these bumpkins for not sailing!" Still not through venting his frustration, he paraphrased a popular ditty:

> *There are, unless my memory fail,*
> *Five causes why we should not sail;*
> *The fog is thick, the wind is high;*
> *It rains, or may do by and by;*
> *Or—any other reason why!*

And there were still people who tried to stop him from preaching. Mobs often sprung up, prompted by local powers. Many were unwilling miners or bargemen or dock workers, prodded by their bosses. John often would determine the leader of the mob and actually take the man by the hand while he reasoned with the rest of the crowd. The effect was nothing short of miraculous. Invariably, the leader instantly transformed into John's fiercest defender.

John rarely was hurt. But not all escaped the wrath of mobs. Some Methodists were pummeled.

All the while, he tirelessly worked the triangle defined by his Methodist centers in London, Bristol and Newcastle. Naturally, he preached most often at those three centers. But he ventured into nearly every shire. In 1747, he began the year in Bristol, then moved on to London. In February, he made the hellish trip through ice and snow north to Newark-on-the-Trent in Lincolnshire. From March to April, he preached in Newcastle, Yorkshore and the Midlands. In June, he returned to London and Bristol, with some time spent also in Plymouth. In July, he was in southwest England at Cornwall. In August, he preached in Wales and made a short trip to Ireland. In September, he returned to Wales and then London.

No one but John himself knew where and when he had been to this village or that. Within the general route he planned ahead of time, his preaching was often spontaneous. In March 1747, he rode from Newcastle up a valley winding through snow-capped mountains. After twenty miles, he reached a decaying town called Blanchard. He stood on a tombstone by a ruined cathedral. Soon, lead miners and their families gathered. Later, he wrote in his journal:

> *A row of little children sat under the oppo-*
> *site wall [of the ruins], all quiet and still.*
> *The whole congregation drank in every word*
> *with such earnestness in their looks, I could*
> *not but hope that God will make this wilder-*
> *ness sing for joy.*

His schedule was staggering. For example, in one week of April of that same year, he preached fifteen times in thirteen different places. He had preached one thousand sermons a year for almost ten years now.

Enthusiasts had asked him about starting societies in Ireland and Scotland. John had tested the water in Ireland and it seemed promising. Scotland was a different matter. Although the land of the Scots was a mere step and a jump away from Newcastle for a traveling man like John, he had no intention of preaching there. Everyone knew the Scots were fiercely attached to Presbyterianism.

"If you spoke like an angel, no Scot would hear you," warned his old friend George Whitefield.

In 1748, John began to preach extensively in Ireland. It

seemed a fierce country to him. "I fear God still has a controversy with this land," he said, "because it is defiled with blood." But the Irish were warmhearted, and John could not stay away. He disembarked at Dublin to preach. Then he traveled west into Ireland's Central Plain until he reached the great River Shannon. Often he was sick on this trip, but he always rallied enough to preach or travel. He preached at Kinnegad, Killcock, Edenderry, Tullamore, Clara and Athlone. Then he retraced his route to Dublin.

In England once again, he conducted the annual conference. As always, someone asked John if the Methodists were going to leave the Church of England. He emphatically denied it, but the question must have been constantly discussed in the societies. Many did not go to the Church of England; they had no way of getting the sacraments.

The conferees then discussed another very important issue: marriage. For some time, both John and Charles were convinced by Saint Paul's advice: it is better for a man of God not to marry. There were other precedents to support celibacy. Many religions denied marriage to those in Holy Orders. And Count Zinzendorf, the founder of the Moravians, having fallen in love with a woman, searched his soul and renounced her, insisting, "My own will is hell to me." Self-denial of such natural pleasure seemed to John and Charles a confirmation of holiness.

But at the Methodist conference of 1748, the other opinion prevailed. Its advocates were so persuasive the two Wesleys themselves were convinced. A preacher could marry and not damage his soul. After all, even though Saint Paul had no wife, Saint Peter did.

One man was very bold. "If the Wesleys were to wed at last, it would certainly put to rest the endless longing of many of the sisters."

John was about to reprimand the man, but stopped. He

had to admit the man was truthful. Many of the sisters did flutter around him and Charles, needlessly, flirtatiously. He often admonished their lack of discipline. How could he have been so blind to their desires?

The Wesleys left the conference changed men. But being methodical, they quickly devised safeguards. The marriage choice of any Methodist leader had to meet the scrutiny of his peers. John and Charles agreed between themselves that neither would marry without the other's "knowledge and consent."

In August, John worked his way north to Newcastle. North of the Midlands, the roads were notoriously rugged. As usual, he read anything he considered worthy as his horse clomped among the ruts and bumps. He had finished writing and distributing his medical book. These days he read Homer's *Iliad,* the ancient Greek classic. He marveled at the author's genius at expression. At times Homer purveyed almost a holy aura, yet often he intermixed the grossest pagan prejudices. Although the Old Testament was older, it was far superior to Homer in moral tone.

"And why not? God's hand guided its scribes," John mused aloud.

In Newcastle, John became very ill. He had been sickly since Ireland. But this ailment seemed the culmination. If he sat up, his head throbbed with pain. If he reclined, he was nauseated. In the night the fever came. Grace Murray nursed him. She seemed to know exactly what to do. She fed him broth. Her feathery, cool hand felt his forehead. She admonished him to sleep.

"You'll be fit in no time, sir." Her voice was pleasant and reassuring.

The next morning, he felt well enough to appreciate Grace. He had so much confidence in her, for once he didn't try to doctor himself. He would write in his journal:

*As a nurse, she is careful to the last degree,
indefatigably patient, and inexpressibly tender. She is quick, cleanly, skillful and under-
stands my constitution better than most
physicians. . . .*

He hadn't felt such comfort since Susanna had mothered
him. Grace was so competent. He blinked his burning eyes
a few times. Had this immaculate angel been up all night?
Her crisp apron looked as if she had just put it on. Her hair
was drawn up, yet not one strand strayed. Her voice was
calm, cheerful.

"You are looking much better, sir," she said.

"If ever I marry, I think you will be the person."

"You flatter me, sir."

She was pleasant and respectful, but her tone dismissed
his comment as that of a sick man. No doubt she heard that
sentiment often. What man nursed by such an obliging
angel wouldn't feel she was almost perfect?

John was startled as he thought about what he had said.
He was always so deliberate. His proposal had popped out,
surely straight from the heart. Did the witness in his heart
speak for him? Very possibly. But he must think on it, too.
What wife could possibly be more of a Christian wife than
Grace? She never complained. She performed her duties
unstintingly. She truly bathed people in agape love. She was
very nearly perfect.

But what of John? He was forty-five. His previous loves
had been failures. Perhaps Sally Kirkham had not been so
disappointed by his reticence. And Kitty Hargreaves seemed
unaffected in the long run by his lack of resolve. But Mary
Pendarves had been hurt by him. And so had Sophy. That last
affair had convinced him he must never encourage any
woman again.

What had changed? Perhaps he had changed a little. But Grace was not like Sophy. Grace was mature. She understood what working for God meant. Surely the two of them would be just about perfect as a Christian couple.

"Grace," he said later, "I do wish to marry you."

"This is too great a blessing for me," she cried. She appeared stunned. She gulped. "This is all I could have wished for under heaven—if I had dared wish for it."

She gave him a strange look, as if waiting for more. But John's mind was racing ahead. The business with Grace was not settled. There was more to be done. He must get Charles's approval. And to make sure his societies did not feel left out, he would compose an exhaustive account of Grace's spiritual qualities. But he couldn't just send it by post. It was too personal. He probably should deliver it to each society. He, of all persons, must abide by their rubrics.

Right now he had more immediate business. Next spring he was returning to Ireland. And he still had to finish his detailed manual on the techniques of preaching. And what about the Christian Library he wanted to compile for the societies?

Charles also was thinking of matrimony. That was no small matter, either. . . .

"Anything else, sir?" Grace asked expectantly. "I should see the other patients."

He returned his attention to Grace. That was just one of the many wonderful things about her. He didn't have to explain every little detail to her. She understood perfectly. A delay would not bother her. After all, she had been widowed for several years and had shown no desire for marriage. Still, he couldn't just leave her so abruptly. That seemed heartless.

"I'm working my way south again with John Bennet," he thought aloud. "You must go with us for a while, Grace."

thirteen

Disappointment

G race Murray did accompany John and Bennet. It was dangerous for all of them, as they found near Roughlee in Lancashire. There a mob finally did hurt John, one man smashing him in the face with his fist. The mob demanded that John never return to Roughlee.

"I would sooner cut off my hand than not return," John answered.

"I won't be any Gamaliel," snarled one man, referring to the wise Jew who encouraged the other Pharisees to tolerate the apostles after Jesus was crucified. "I'll be like Herod and Pilate."

"What an admission," John murmured.

They finally made their escape but were pelted by dirt and rocks. One of the Methodists was thrown into a river. Another was dragged from his horse and beaten. But all survived Roughlee.

Further on, in Bolton, they were mobbed again, but the result was as miraculous as it was disastrous in Roughlee. As John was speaking, stones began to fly in every direction and three men rushed him. One of the men was struck in the ear by a stone and immediately retreated. A stone hit the second man in the forehead and stopped him. The third man's hand was struck just as it was reaching for John. Suddenly, the crowd quieted and let John finish his sermon.

"We were in God's hands today," John told his companions.

"But I see now our opponents have laid many snares for us on this trip. Grace must not be endangered any more."

"Our opponents are spreading rumors about her, too," John Bennet volunteered hotly. "And even our own Methodist people are wondering why she travels with us."

So John had Grace stay behind with Bennet. John had planned to tell her more than he had, but the schedule was so demanding he hadn't done it. He worked his way back to London, where he most often spent the bitter winter months. There he and Charles decided that among three candidates, Charles should wed Sally Gwynn. She lived on an estate at Garth in southeast Wales. Her father Marmaduke Gwynn, a very powerful man, had befriended the Methodists. The whole Gwynn family welcomed them. That area of Wales had become a tranquil oasis to the Wesleys on their preaching jaunts. Yes, Sally was most worthy. In every way John encouraged Charles, who was showing signs of doubt.

Finally, Charles was versing his own optimism:

> *Two are better than one,*
> *For counsel or for fight!*
> *How can man be warm alone*
> *Or serve his God aright?*

On April 8, 1749, Charles Wesley, a bachelor of forty-one, wed Sally Gwynn, a young woman of twenty-two. John performed the ceremony at Garth. All the Gwynns were there: parents, older brother Howell, oldest sister Mary Baldwin and Sally's unmarried siblings: Becky, twenty-four; Joan, twenty; Betsy, eighteen; and Roderick, thirteen. Grace Murray was there, too, because she was going to sail to Ireland with John after the wedding. Charles would take his new wife Sally and her sister Becky to Bristol to live.

On the ship to Ireland, John realized he still had not told Charles about his plan to wed Grace. If only he weren't so busy. He still had to write his exhaustive account of her spiritual qualities for the brothers and sisters, too. And he had been working on his preaching manual. Perhaps he should finish that first—in what little spare time he had. After all, it was more important to the society at large. Could he put himself and Grace before the interests of the society? Hardly.

So he perfected his manual. It was no vague manual. John was a perfectionist. He knew that on a calm day his own voice, speaking conversationally, could be heard about 140 yards away. And how did he know? He and Charles had tested it. In his manual, under the precise heading "How we may speak so as to be heard without difficulty and with pleasure," John wrote :

> *[Speak] just as you do in common conversation. . .with a natural, easy and graceful variation of the voice, suitable to the nature and sentiments to be delivered. . .[words should] flow like a gliding stream, not as a rapid torrent. . . .*

He listed all the don'ts of elocution:

> *[Do not speak] too loudly or too softly. . .too rapidly or too slowly. . .thick, cluttering manner. . .womanish. . .squeaking . . .singing. . .canting. . .swelling. . . theatrical. . .whining. . .whimsical. . . .*

Under a different heading there was the all-important silent language of the face, body, and hands. Every movement should be made with a purpose. Hands and eyes always should act in concert:

> *[The head is] modestly and decently upright.*
> *. . .[Eyes meet the eyes of listeners] with an*
> *air of affection and regard. . . .[Never stretch*
> *arms] sideways more than half a foot [from*
> *the] trunk of the body. . . .*
> *The preacher should never clap or pound the*
> *pulpit. He should use the right hand more fre-*
> *quently than the left. He should not move the*
> *body incessantly or jerkily. There should be*
> *no emotional contortions of the face. . . .*

He read what he had written to Grace. "Do you think this is exhaustive enough?"

"I hadn't realized it was so premeditated."

John pondered a while. "I think it needs more work. We mustn't have weak preachers. And that reminds me, I still need to translate *Martin Luther's Life* from German into English for our school children. I plan to provide them with a basic Christian Library, much of which I must translate or condense."

Grace blinked. "You are so busy, sir."

"You understand me so well, Grace."

And John wrote in his journal:

> *The more we conversed together, the more I*
> *loved her. . . .She was to me both a servant*
> *and a friend, as well as a fellow laborer in*
> *the Gospel.*

When they returned to England after several weeks in Ireland, Grace seemed anxious to return to Newcastle. *It was little wonder,* John thought. Some gossip had surfaced about her among the sisters, which was very unfair and disgusting. And the dear woman was so dedicated to her work at Newcastle. He had kept her from it. No doubt she would be absorbed in it for some time to come. That would give him time to discuss his plans for marriage with Charles. And he still must write of her spiritual qualities for the brothers and sisters. And there were a few matters to clear up in Newcastle —the few trifling complaints he had heard about Grace.

But in the meantime, the great summer event was approaching. "I can't be unprepared for the conference," he reminded himself.

To his amazement, he realized after the conference he still had not told Charles of his plans to marry. Then he received news that shook him like a bombshell: John Bennet and Grace were planning to marry!

John rushed to Grace. "But we were betrothed!" he complained.

"I don't know what to do. I've waited for you for quite some time."

John talked her into becoming his fiancée again. Correspondence began among John, Bennet, and Grace. None of the three wanted to hurt anyone. John assured her he would soon take his forty-six-page evaluation of her spiritual qualities around to the societies. He already had investigated the complaints about her in Newcastle; they were indeed trivial. Then he remembered Charles. He still had not told him. He would get around to it.

"No regrets then?" he asked Grace as he left her to keep his busy schedule.

"None at all, sir."

At Whitehaven, on the northwest coast of England, John was surprised by none other than Charles himself. He had never seen Charles so breathless, so upset, so livid.

"You've betrayed me!" Charles seethed. "With that common woman!"

"Have you discovered my intentions to marry Grace Murray?"

"Certainly. Didn't you write John Bennet? Haven't you been talking to everyone in the society about her?"

"I was going to talk to you."

"Now you can."

John explained his intentions and Charles answered him with a list of objections. People were already saying it would tear the societies apart, Charles insisted. And she would slow John's work. And many felt John had stolen her from Bennet. She had nursed Bennet for several weeks once, before John's illness. Did John not know that?

"What?" John interrupted. "Do you think this is a series of sickbed romances with a nurse?"

"Many think she was betrothed to Bennet, and you used your superior position to coerce her into breaking her vow to him."

John blinked. "Perhaps it is more complicated than I knew. Why don't we have an arbiter, then? Vincent Perronet, the vicar of Shoreham? You trust his judgment, don't you?"

"Certainly."

"In the meantime, I'll write my reasons down, backed by Scripture."

So John labored that evening over his reasons for marriage. The annual conference of 1748 had removed his theological objections, but he discussed them anyway. Charles had declared that Grace was too common for John. John dismissed that in a flash. He really had only to justify Grace on practical reasons. The marriage would add no expense because Grace already worked for the Methodists. Any children from their marriage could be educated at their school in Kingswood, near Bristol. Other advantages were that Grace was an excellent housekeeper, nurse, companion, friend, and laborer for Christ. And contrary to tearing the societies apart, she would put to rest certain divisive temptations:

> *She would guard many [women] from inordinate affection for me, to which they would be far less exposed, both because they would have far less hope of success, and because I should converse far more sparingly with them; perhaps not in private with any young woman at all; at least not with any member of our own societies.*

John surveyed his detailed list of thirty-two propositions. They ended with two conclusions: 1) John had scriptural reason to marry and 2) no person was so proper for him as Grace Murray. "How I love to analyze," he admitted. "But the reasons are irrefutable."

The next day John could not find Charles. He had disappeared. By afternoon the truth had hit John. Charles had gone to see Grace in Lindley Hill. It was less than a day's ride from Whitehaven, but because of John's late start he had to meander through mist and bogs on a moonless night. He became lost several times before the mist cleared. Then, navigating by starlight, he drove his horse right through the bogs. It was the next morning before he arrived at the house in Lindley Hill where Grace had been staying.

The host rushed out. "Grace left with your brother!"

John was stunned. Should he follow them? Where had

they gone? To Newcastle? Where? No one was sure. And he turned back. Later in Whitehaven he wrote in his journal:

> *. . .If I had more regard for her I loved, than for the work of God, I should now have gone on straight to Newcastle and not back to Whitehaven. I knew this was giving up all. But I knew God called. . . .*

A few days later, John learned what Charles had done. He had taken Grace to John Bennet and exhorted them to marry. They had! John was furious with Charles, but worse, he was stung to the core of his soul by Grace's willingness to marry Bennet. The fury and hurt cooled to a dull ache of resentment toward both Charles and Grace.

George Whitefield, who had been preaching to the societies once more, invited John to Leeds to reconcile with everyone involved. Before Charles arrived in Leeds, John learned Whitefield had begged Charles not to abort John's plans with Grace Murray. John was angry again. Then Charles burst in on John and Whitefield, not conciliatory at all but angry and abusive. Yet, in a surprisingly short time the brothers reconciled.

The truth was that John could not be hurt any more than he already had been. And in his heart he knew now he had treated Charles unfairly, insisting to the last jot and tittle on helping Charles select a wife, then leaving Charles completely out of the selection of his own wife.

But when Grace arrived with Bennet, John revealed once again how hurt he was. Only a long, heartfelt appeal by Charles and Whitefield could persuade him to see the married couple. John would rather have faced a mob with their stones and clubs. On his way to Newcastle later, John poured out his anguish:

> *Oh Lord, I bow my sinful head!*
> *Righteous are all Thy ways with man.*
> *Yet suffer me with Thee to plead,*
> *With lowly reverence to complain:*
> *With deep unuttered grief to groan,*
> *Oh what is this that Thou hast done?*

He continued purging his hurt in stanza after stanza. Yes, John was a sinner, and God was righteous, but what was the purpose of all this pain?

In the weeks that followed, John recovered from the loss of Grace Murray. It was the meddling of Charles, however well-founded, that haunted him. Even if John had wronged him, was Charles justified in such drastic interference? It was almost as if the ghost of his well-intentioned father Samuel was meddling in his life again.

Only John's societies satisfied him. Here, he was living in Christ. He was sure of that. And it was his calling. In ten years, he had built a network of thousands of Methodists laboring for Christ in England and Ireland. There had never been such an organization devoted to holiness in England, with its local societies, with class meetings, with circuit riders, with an annual conference. Wasn't building and administering such labor for Christ satisfaction enough? Hadn't God blessed him beyond all his desires? Wasn't happiness to be found only in holiness?

Days after the turmoil, he would write:

> *I rode to Birmingham. . . . Such a congrega-*
> *tion I never saw there before: not a scoffer,*
> *nor a trifler, not an inattentive person. . .*

167

among them; and seldom have I known so deep, solemn a sense of the power, and presence, and love of God. . . .

In March 1750, he sailed once again for Ireland. He had a respectable number of societies started there already, the Dublin society swelling to more than four hundred members. He worked hard in Ireland, once riding ninety miles in one day. Dogs were let loose on him. Mobs jeered him. But the work continued.

Back in England once again, he learned Hetty had died in London. She had been an invalid for years, believing every day was her last. In 1743, she had written John, "Now my health is gone" and "I have been so long weak that I know not how long my trial may last." Of her surviving two brothers and four sisters, only Charles was at her graveside when she was buried. She had written her own epitaph:

DESTINED WHILE LOVING TO SUSTAIN
AN EQUAL SHARE OF GRIEF AND PAIN:
ALL VARIOUS ILLS OF HUMAN RACE
WITHIN THIS BREAST HAD ONCE A PLACE.
WITHOUT COMPLAINT SHE LEARNED TO BEAR,
A LIVING DEATH, A LONG DESPAIR;
TILL HARD OPPRESSED BY ADVERSE FATE,
O'ERCHARGED, SHE SUNK BENEATH ITS WEIGHT;
AND TO THIS PEACEFUL TOMB RETIRED,
SO MUCH ESTEEMED, SO LONG DESIRED.
THE PAINFUL MORTAL CONFLICTS O'ER;
A BROKEN HEART CAN BLEED NO MORE!

Hetty was not being melodramatic. Her poor husband had fought alcoholism their entire marriage. She was in severe pain at the end. She had lost all her babies. John had her many poems, and he vowed one day somehow he would have them published. Most were as bittersweet as the opening lines of the poem she wrote for one of her dying babies:

> *Tender softness! Infant mild!*
> *Perfect, sweetest, loveliest child!*
> *Transient luster! Beauteous clay!*
> *Smiling wonder of a day!*

John rejoiced that for Hetty's last years she had found her Savior through the Methodists and "she was at rest before she went hence."

In London, John was surprised at the entreaties of two close friends, banker Ebenezer Blackwell and Vincent Perronet, the vicar of Shoreham—the very man John had proposed as arbiter in the Grace Murray affair. Both men were very upset at the chasm growing between John and Charles. Both were even more concerned about John's loneliness. Their solution was simple: they had found the perfect wife for John. She was Molly Vazeille, a wealthy, forty-year-old widow of a banker. Her four children were grown. Best of all, they said, Charles knew her. She had not only stayed at the Gwynns' estate in Wales, but Charles and his wife Sally had stayed at Mrs. Vazeille's house in London on Threadneedle Street.

"I'll think on it," John said, still smarting from yet another of his failures in humanly love. And there was a nagging thought that Charles might be behind this matchmaking. Was Mary Vazeille his choice?

That September, John spent much time at his school in Kingswood. He had not neglected the Christian Library for his students, but much remained to be done. So he selected passages by Milton for students to transcribe and recite weekly. For other reading, he condensed books on Greek antiquity, Hebrew antiquity, primitive Christianity, English history, Roman history, and Latin grammar. William Law and John Bunyan were read by older students.

As the air turned bitter, John headed back to London for the winter. In January 1751, John risked the icy roads to visit Oxford, where he was perplexed by the esteem shown him. Had he at last become respectable? It didn't seem normal not to be laughed at, pointed at, or called names. And for a moment, he was sorely tempted to stay there, once again a fellow, in peace and quiet, to analyze and discuss with clever peers. But the temptation passed.

On the icy road back to London, the entreaties about marriage by Perronet and Blackwell weighed on him. A thought struck him: "Did I reject my fellowship again in an unconscious desire to clear the way for marriage?" After all, he had thoroughly assessed marriage and found it most acceptable for himself and the societies.

Ice caught up with John in London. Crossing London Bridge on February 10, he fell, injuring his ankle. Remarkably, he convalesced not at the Foundry—but at Mrs. Vazeille's house on Threadneedle Street! It was Ebenezer Blackwell's idea. And the doting widow quickly won John's heart. She was so kind and attentive, just like Grace. She certainly had the advantage over Grace in education and manners. She could discuss many refined things.

Should he marry her? She was very intelligent, but there was a hint she might be sharp-tongued like Sammy's wife. But as Blackwell reminded him, Methodists are blunt. And Molly was only a budding Methodist, sure to become mellower just as John had mellowed himself.

So to John's amazement, he proposed again—but he was more cautious this time. "Of course, I'll have to discuss this with brother Charles first," he told her.

"I accept your proposal, but urge you to proceed immediately."

"Why, dear lady?"

"It's common knowledge that your brother will not approve any marriage for you."

"Not so common that I know it," he snapped.

But the more he thought about it, the more he tended to agree with Molly. Perhaps he would not tell Charles. What if Charles wasn't behind any of this? John couldn't endure another emotional storm like the last one. And deep in his heart, he realized he had not forgiven Charles for meddling. John would wait and announce his marriage at the chapel in the Foundry the day before they wed.

And so he did. On February 18, 1751, John's friend Charles Manning wed John to Mary Vazeille in Middlesex, north of London. Charles refused to attend. Worse, he sent word he would not be attending the annual conference in Bristol!

"He's lazy," Molly said. "And why should he get more compensation per year than you?"

Thus, John not only knew Charles was not behind any of this matchmaking, but he began to suspect Charles and Molly were mutually antagonistic. The days ahead proved him right.

And he began to see how flawed Molly was: prideful, spiteful, materialistic, gossipy. What had he done? He had delayed his affections for years with Sally Kirkham, Mrs. Pendarves, Kitty Hargreaves, Sophy Hopkey and Grace Murray, as he agonized endlessly over their qualities. Now he had plunged headlong into marriage with a woman he barely knew.

After the conference in Bristol, he had to travel north to Newcastle. He told his wife, "A Methodist preacher can not answer to God if he preaches one sermon less or travels one day less in a married state than in a single state."

"What am I to do?" she asked coldly.

"You have two choices. For nine months you can live here in London just as you have the last few years, and I will be here the other three months. Or you can travel with me."

She did not want to leave Threadneedle Street.

Later that year, John took his first trip to Scotland. He was very impressed with the towns and inns and cleanliness. It was obvious the English lied about Scotland, bitter over their eternal squabbles over royal matters. But the Scots were not receptive to John's preaching. It was as George Whitefield had said once: The Scots "know everything and feel nothing."

John's relationship with wife Molly consisted of three months of intimacy in London, followed by nine months of loving, heartfelt letters. That was in harmony with the Great Commission, so it was sufficient for John. But it was not for Molly. She changed her mind about traveling with John, but she was in no way like the selfless, humble Grace Murray. . . .

fourteen

Conflicts

After traveling with wife Molly a few times, John was to write in exasperation:

In my last journey north all my patience was put to the proof, again and again. . . .I am content with whatever. . .I meet with. . .and this must be the spirit of all who take journeys with me. If a dinner ill-dressed, a hard bed, a poor room, a shower of rain or a dirty road, will put them out of humor, it lays a burden on me. . . .To have such persons at my ear, fretting and murmuring at everything, it is like tearing the flesh off my bones. . . .

In Ireland in fall 1752, Molly reached the end of her rope. The vicious weather, angry mobs, and endless meetings aggravated her. Her unkempt appearance at reaching such meetings humiliated and enraged her. Finally, in a fury she attacked John in the room where they were sleeping that night. It was no match. John was strong and wiry though small, but his downfall was pacifism. He merely tried to fend her off as she grabbed and clawed and punched. Any intimacy in the marriage was over. There would be no children.

Although John's activity never slowed, he fought bitter thoughts. His wife seemed no better than an enemy now. And Charles distressed him, too. His brother was more and more distant, and his preaching jaunts were not just independent but secretive. In exasperation, John wrote him in October 1753:

> . . . .*Either act really in connection with me, or never pretend it. Rather disclaim it, and openly avow you do and will not. By acting in connection with me, I mean take counsel with me once or twice a year as to the places where you will labor. Hear my advice before you fix [your destinations], whether you take it or not. At present you are so far from this that I do not even know when and where you intend to go. . . .*

Soon, John had a more pressing problem: his health. At Leigh in November 1753, he preached in weather so cold he felt he was standing in ice water. Day after day he was drawn into situations that chilled him to the bones. Finally, he returned to London with pain in his left lung, a racking cough and low fever. He recovered quickly and began to preach again. But the recovery was an illusion. The symptoms returned, stronger than ever. His left lung throbbed pain and he now had a rattling cough. Bed rest was the wisest course, but John refused to miss scheduled engagements. By the third week of his illness, a well-respected physician insisted he stop preaching. "Go to the country to rest!" the physician demanded.

For once, John was too weak to ride a horse. A coach took him to Ebenezer Blackwell's estate in Lewisham. There he lay in bed, feverish and hurting. Rest seemed impossible with the cough. He had a dread infection called "galloping consumption." It was usually fatal.

This was a black moment for John—as bad as the worst storm at sea. Charles had drifted away from him. His wife was a vicious, jealous tyrant. And now this disease. John was just fifty, with a thousand things left to do—but dying. Was he afraid? How could he be? Paradise could come at any moment.

Ever methodical, he wrote his own epitaph, fearing one that would be too sentimental or laudatory:

HERE LIETH THE BODY

OF

JOHN WESLEY

A BRAND PLUCKED OUT OF THE BURNING

WHO DIED OF A CONSUMPTION

IN THE FIFTY-FIRST YEAR

OF HIS AGE,

NOT LEAVING, AFTER HIS DEBTS ARE PAID,

TEN POUNDS BEHIND HIM:

PRAYING,

GOD BE MERCIFUL TO ME, AN UNPROFITABLE

SERVANT!

He carefully added at the bottom "He ordered that this, if any, inscription should be placed on his tombstone."

Too bad John didn't know his exact worth. Before his marriage, he had renounced any claim to his wife's wealth. His printing debts were enormous. Perhaps he was in debt, after all. Still, the epitaph was close enough. It was very important for a Methodist minister to die with almost nothing. Now he could relax a bit, which meant praying or reading or thinking.

He prayed for a while, then he thought. This illness was not like the ones in 1741 and 1747. He'd had a fever in those illnesses, too, but this illness was a very serious lung ailment. It was obvious the medications prescribed by his physician were not working. If he were to use his own home medical book, what would he try? Sulfur might work. He had a plaster made of sulfur and egg white on brown paper, and had his left side wrapped.

"God, help me, if it is your will," he said hopefully.

175

Five minutes later, the pain in his lung was gone. In half an hour, he had no fever. He felt stronger by the minute. His ministry would continue.

It took several weeks to recover. But John was not idle. He condensed books for the Christian Library for his students. Then he began a work he admitted would never have been done except for his illness: notes on the New Testament.

To his sorrow, he learned his brother Charles had his own problems in Bristol. Sally had smallpox. For more than thirty years in England, a medical technique called inoculation had been said to prevent severe smallpox. A person intentionally was infected by another with a very mild case of smallpox. It was dangerous, though, and Sally had not done it. Now John learned she was going to recover—praise God—but was badly scarred. Then disaster truly struck: their only child, eighteen-month-old Jacky, named for John, caught the disease and died.

When John traveled to Hot Wells near Bristol for further recuperation, he spent more time with Charles than he had in many years. John thanked God he was with Charles. Charles was suffering profound grief. When his son was alive, Charles was afraid to love him too much, as if he would not have enough love left for God. Now he wrote:

> *Dead! Dead! The child I loved so well!*
> *Transported to the world above!*
> *I need no more my heart conceal:*
> *I never dared indulge my love:*
> *But may I not indulge my grief,*
> *And seek in tears a sad relief?*

John's sickness unsettled the societies. Charles was known to suffer periodic serious illnesses, but John's near fatal illness was a shock. When he finally preached again, it was after an absence of four months! By that time, every Methodist from Cornwall to Newcastle was speculating on the question of leaving the Church of England if the Wesleys were not there to hold them.

The 1755 conference at Leeds brought the question to the forefront. For three days, the sixty-three leaders discussed separating from the church. The probing was civil on all sides. A few wanted to separate because they disagreed with church doctrine. Many wanted to separate because of the hostility they encountered in their parish churches; some were refused Holy Communion. John's own opinion was that he wished to stay within the Church of England, and it was fully legal within church doctrine to field preach, to pray without the *Book of Common Prayer,* to form Methodist societies, and to allow preaching by those not ordained by bishops.

Then John concluded, "Before I will surrender any of those four activities, I will quit the Church of England!"

Charles was astounded. He now was convinced John was leading the societies away from the church. In turn, during the next few years, Charles seemed to withdraw more and more —not only from the societies, but from John's control. He had not traveled to Ireland since 1749. By 1757, he was no longer an itinerant preacher. He faithfully managed the Methodist center in Bristol. But he was resentful of John's dominance, even indiscreetly speaking of breaking his bondage.

John's marriage had deteriorated more. What had been a quarrelsome, unhappy bond became vicious and tormented. The catalyst was his matron at Kingswood school, Mrs. Sarah Ryan. She was in her thirties, with a long, involved history of being tricked and abused by men. Her first husband turned out to be a bigamist. Her next husband was a sailor lost at sea who returned after she had married again. Now she had no one at all. John sympathized with her troubles. His wife Molly did not.

"What is all this correspondence from Mrs. Ryan?" she demanded.

"Many brothers and sisters correspond with me."

"Even a tramp with three living husbands?"

In January 1758, Molly found an unsealed letter he had

written to Mrs. Ryan in his coat pocket. It apologized for Molly's insolent behavior toward members of the society, especially the courageous Mrs. Ryan. But the sentence that drove Molly into jealous rage read, "The conversing with you, either by speaking or writing, is an unspeakable blessing to me." In a fury, Molly left John.

Not all the societies ran smoothly. The one at Norwich, in the watery Norfolk Broads, had been particularly troublesome. The people there were as stubborn and independent as the Fensmen. John and Charles had to visit Norwich in 1753 to rein in its renegade preacher James Wheatley. His doctrine was unintelligible. After many warnings, they had to expel him. A few years later, John was in Norwich again. This time their preachers were giving the sacraments, which Methodist preachers were not supposed to perform outside the Church of England.

Later, John told Charles, "I told them they were the most ignorant, self-conceited, self-willed, fickle, untractable, disorderly, disjointed society that I knew in the three kingdoms of England, Ireland and Scotland!"

"And how did they take it?" Charles asked dryly.

"Not one was offended."

Methodism was past its twentieth year, and prospering. Charles and Sally had another son, Charles Junior, still healthy. John's marriage continued to crumble. But after all, he and Molly were only human.

It hadn't been long since John was in the robe chamber off the House of Lords, watching King George the Second himself. John adored the seventy-three-year-old king. He was hard-working and proved himself loyal and brave at the Battle of Dettingen. His clever helpmate of a wife Caroline had now been dead for two decades. Later John wrote:

His brow was much furrowed with age, and
quite clouded with care. And is this all the
world can give even to a king? [Is this] all

> *the grandeur it can afford? A blanket of
> ermine round his shoulders, so heavy and
> cumbersome he can scarce move under it! A
> huge heap of borrowed hair, with a few
> plates of gold and glittering stones upon his
> head! Alas, what a bauble is human great-
> ness! And even this will not endure. . . .*

Nor did the king endure, dying in 1760. Only God and his
Kingdom endure, John praised. So he shepherded his flock,
always exhorting, always admonishing. He wanted to im-
prove every local society and every individual in the ways of
God. Piety could not be neglected. He wrote of one society:

> *A few months ago the generality of people in
> these parts were exceedingly lifeless. Samuel
> Meggot. . .advised the society. . .to observe
> every Friday with fasting and prayer. The
> very first Friday. . .God broke in upon them in
> a wonderful manner; and His work has been
> increasing among them ever since. The
> neighboring societies. . .agreed to follow the
> same rule, and soon experienced the same
> blessing. Is not the neglect of this plain duty
> (I mean fasting, ranked by our Lord with
> almsgiving and prayer) one general occasion
> of deadness among Christians? Can any one
> neglect it, and be guiltless?*

Another thing bothered him:

> *I am more convinced than ever that the
> preaching like an Apostle, without joining
> together those that are weakened, and train-
> ing them up in the ways of God, is only beget-
> ting children for the murderer. How much*

179

preaching has there been for these twenty years all over Pembrokeshire! But no regular societies, no discipline, no order or connection; and the consequence is that. . .the once-awakened are now faster asleep than ever.

And always there was the grinding travel. One day in 1764 was one of the most maddening in his many journeys.

I took a horse a little after four and about two preached in the market-place of Llanidloes [about 40] miles from Shrewsbury. At three we rode through the mountains to Fountainhead. . . .We mounted again about seven. [We became lost and] ended in the edge of a bog. . . .An honest man, instantly mounting his horse, galloped before us, up hill and down, till he brought us into a road, which he said led straight to Roes-fair. We rode on, till another [man] met us, and said, "No, this is the way to Aberystwith. . . .You must turn back and ride to that yonder bridge. The master of the little house near the bridge directed us to the next village. . . .[Later, it being past nine,] having wandered an hour upon the mountain, through rocks, and bogs, and precipices, we. . .got back to the little house near the bridge. . .[the house now] being full of drunken, roaring miners; besides that, there was not one bed in the house, and neither grass nor hay nor corn. . . .We hired one of [the miners] to walk with us to Roes-fair, though he was miserably drunk, till falling all his length in a purling stream, he came tolerably to his senses. Between eleven and twelve we came to the inn. . . .[The next

> *morning we found] the mule was cut in sev-*
> *eral places and my mare was bleeding like a*
> *pig, from a wound. . .made, it seems, by. . .a*
> *pitchfork. . . .*

And always there were intensely personal family matters. Sister Sukey died in December 1764 after years of evading her alcoholic husband. She was sixty-nine. Charles and Sally lost more infants; of six children, they had lost four. These tragedies were expected, but never easy. Sister Patty had ten children, of whom only one lived past infancy—and that boy died at fourteen from smallpox. Death was never far away. George Whitefield, only fifty, and eleven years younger than John, was looking very old and haggard.

Yet the societies slowly grew—although John cared nothing for numbers, but only for righteousness. By 1765, the societies embraced thirty-nine circuits administered by ninety-two preachers. Membership totaled more than twenty thousand.

In 1769, somewhat defensively because of unending opposition, he wrote to a woman his criteria for "Christian perfection":

1. *Loving God with all our heart. Do you object to this?*
2. *A heart and life all devoted to God. Do you desire less?*
3. *Regaining the whole image of God. What objection to this?*
4. *Having all the mind that was in Christ. Is this going too far?*
5. *Walking uniformly as Christ walked. This surely no Christian will object to.*
   If any one means anything less or else by perfection, I have no concern with it. . . .What need of this heat about it, this violence. . .fury of opposition. . . ?

At the 1769 conference in Leeds, one hundred and eleven leaders took up what seemed a small order of business. Some members of Methodist societies had immigrated to America. They had tried to keep their Methodism alive there. One group in New York was so dedicated as to build a small meeting house. But now these faithful were asking John Wesley for preachers.

The cause in New York was aided by an English officer, Capt. Thomas Webb, whom John remembered and respected. The conferees responded by sending preachers Richard Boardman and Richard Pilmoor to America. And why not? The colonists were an extension of England. The new preachers were soon to report that New York and Philadelphia each had one hundred members.

The year 1770 was sad for John. George Whitefield died in America. On the other hand, John himself never felt better. On his sixty-seventh birthday, he reflected on his health:

> *I can hardly believe that I am this day entered into the sixty-eighth year of my age. How marvelous are the ways of God! How has He kept me even from a child! From ten to thirteen or fourteen, I had little but bread to eat, and not great plenty of that. I believe this was so far from hurting me, that it laid the foundation of lasting health. When I grew up, in consequence of reading Dr. Cheyne, I chose to eat sparingly, and drink water. This was another great means of continuing my health, till. . .I was afterwards brought to the brink of death by a fever; but it left me healthier than before. . . .Years after, I was in the third stage of consumption (1753). . . .It pleased God to remove this also. Since that time I have known neither pain nor sickness, am now healthier than I was forty years ago. This hath God wrought!*

Sister Emily died at seventy-nine in 1771. Of the once large family, only the two brothers and sisters Patty and Anne survived. Patty was now living at the Foundry. She had become part of the famous intellectual circle around Samuel Johnson. To a lesser degree, so had Charles. John met occasionally with Johnson, too, but the stay was always brief.

"You talk well on any subject," Johnson enthused. "Cross your legs and stay a while longer."

"Pardon me, sir, but I am obliged to meet with a widow and her family in an hour," John explained. "I must go."

"You are always in a hurry, sir," Johnson complained.

"No, sir. I am always in haste, but never in a hurry. I never undertake more than I can do with perfect calmness of spirit."

Of eight infants, Charles and Sally now had three children surviving. Charles Junior was fourteen, Sally twelve and Sammy five. Both boys were musical prodigies, and Charles longed to have them studying music in London. But to most Methodists, the pursuit of an art like classical music was considered frivolous.

The Charles Wesley family became very unpopular with the Methodists in Bristol. So supported by a wealthy patron, Charles moved his family into the patron's four-story Georgian mansion on Chesterfield Street in London. Although officially Charles pastored the chapels at the Foundry and West Street, it seemed to John that Charles had taken one more step away from Methodism.

John's marriage still limped along. Occasionally they reconciled, but it never lasted. After Molly had left him again, in his journal John noted sourly in Latin: *"Non eam reliqui; non dimisi; non revocabo,"* which translated "I did not desert her; I did not dismiss her; I will not recall her." Molly's personal wealth was a double-edged sword to John. Yes, it made her independent and spoiled, but it also gave her the means to stay away from him.

By 1771, the Methodists in America were still clamoring for preachers. How could they spread the Gospel in an entire continent with just two preachers? So John sent two more preachers to America, one of whom was Francis Asbury, twenty-six, from the area of Wednesbury where John once had been mobbed. The two new preachers took the societies in Philadelphia and New York, allowing the first two to venture north and south.

By the time the American Methodists held their first conference in Philadelphia in 1773, they numbered ten preachers and more than eleven hundred members! But as promising as America seemed now for Methodism, it also seemed ripe for turmoil. The colonists seemed to resent every intrusion by the king's authority. And King George the Third was determined to assert his authority. His prime minister, Lord North, was heavy-handed, too, enraging the colonists with new taxes. An incident in Boston between colonists and English troops resulted in the deaths of several colonists. Was this storm going to scatter the flock in America?

By 1774, John's personal life became even stormier.

fifteen

Separations

"If Molly lives a thousand years twice over, she can't undo her evil mischief," John sputtered.

"What is it?" replied brother Charles.

"Molly has gone public."

In an effort to disgrace John, his wife had released his personal letters to the newspapers. But they were not intact originals. They were copies with sections interpolated to make John look as dishonest and hypocritical as possible. John was now seventy years old, faced with unremitting opposition from his own bitter wife. And what could he do? How his enemies reveled in the letters!

One emboldened enemy, George Sutherland, pressed false charges against John and had him arrested. But when a magistrate tried the case he was so incensed at the fabrications he acquitted John and fined Sutherland a thousand pounds!

And there were the ever-present hazards of travel. In the rugged countryside near Newcastle, John was riding in a carriage with a woman and her two small girls when the horses bolted for no reason at all, throwing the driver from the carriage. Driverless, the carriage careened down a hill, missed a cart, crossed a narrow bridge, entered a farmer's yard, crashed through a gate, then lurched wildly through a field of wheat before stopping at the brink of a high cliff. During the entire episode, John felt no more fear than he would have felt while sitting by a fireside reading a book.

"I am convinced," he told the woman and her two small girls as the dust settled, "that both good angels and evil spirits shared this adventure with us."

Days later, when he turned seventy-one, he once more marveled at his excellent health in his journal:

> . . . .*My sight is considerably better now, and my nerves firmer, than they were [thirty years ago]. . . .The grand cause is, the good pleasure of God, who doeth whatsoever pleaseth Him. The chief means are: 1. My constantly rising at four, for about fifty years. 2. My generally preaching at five in the morning, one of the most healthy exercises in the world. 3. My never traveling less, by sea or land, than four thousand five hundred miles in a year.*

Meanwhile, the situation in America was approaching full-scale war. John was very worried. While he was in Ireland in June 1775, confined to a sickbed, he heard muddled reports of much bloodshed at Concord, Massachusetts, between British regulars and colonial militiamen. Lord North, the prime minister, seemed determined to bring the colonists to their knees. From his sickbed, John wrote Lord North to implore him to keep peace:

> . . . .*I would not speak, as it may seem to be concerning myself with things that lie out of my province. But I dare not refrain from it any longer; I think silence in the present case would be a sin against God, against my country, and against my soul. . . .I do not intend to enter upon the question whether the Americans*

are in the right or in the wrong. Here all my prejudices are against the Americans; for I am a High Churchman, the son of a High Churchman, bred up from my childhood on the highest notions of passive obedience and non-resistance. And yet, in spite of all my long-rooted prejudices, I cannot avoid thinking, if I think at all, these, an oppressed people, asked for nothing more than their legal rights, and that in the most modest and inoffensive manner. . . .But waiving. . .all consideration of right and wrong, I ask, is it common sense to use force toward the Americans? A letter now before me. . .says "Four hundred of the regulars and forty of the militia were killed in the late skirmish. . . ." You see, my Lord, whatever has been affirmed, these men will not be frightened. And it seems they will not be conquered so easily as was at first imagined. They will probably dispute every inch of ground, and, if they die, die sword in hand. Indeed, some of our valiant officers say, "Two thousand men will clear America of these rebels." No, nor twenty thousand, be they rebels or not, nor perhaps treble that number. They are as strong men as you; they are as valiant as you, if not abundantly more valiant, for they are one and all enthusiasts—enthusiasts for liberty. . . .We know men animated with this spirit will leap into a fire or rush into a cannon's mouth. . . .What an advantage they have over many that fight only for pay. . . .Have they not another considerable advantage? . . .

187

> *Their supplies are at hand and all round them;*
> *ours are three thousand miles off! But my*
> *Lord, this is not all. . . .As I travel four or five*
> *thousand miles every year I have an opportu-*
> *nity of conversing freely. . . .I cannot but know*
> *the general disposition of the people—*
> *English, Scots, and Irish; and I know a large*
> *majority of them are exasperated almost to*
> *madness. . . .*

So John argued both the moral and the practical sides. He felt he knew what the ruling class did not know: that their own British commoners, short of all life's necessities, would bitterly resent the king's expenditure on this foreign venture.

But within days, still sick, John had digested his friend Samuel Johnson's pamphlet "Taxation No Tyranny," which was directed against the Americans. John was convinced once again of the king's rightful authority and now advanced Johnson's argument in his own pamphlet "A Calm Address to our American Colonies."

"If no one else in England would understand my mixed signals, brother Charles would," John told his friends in Ireland. "He would know I'm worried about the terrible effects of war. He knows there is great resentment against the king right now among our own people. Yet he also knows I am completely loyal to the king. And my brother knows I can't lie in bed and do nothing."

Lord North continued his oppressive measures. A Virginian named George Washington was picked to lead the American resistance. The Methodist preachers were now in jeopardy. It was very dangerous to move about the countryside. If a young man was not in one army or the other, he might be considered a spy. But John urged his preachers to refrain from choosing sides:

*You were never in your lives in so critical a
situation as you are at this time. It is your
part to be peacemakers, to be loving and
tender to all, but to addict yourself to no
party. . .say not one word against one or the
other side. Keep yourselves pure, do all you
can to help and soften all. . . .*

But when the Americans declared their independence one
year later in 1776 and war seemed inevitable, John had to
urge his preachers to return to England. Only Francis Asbury
stayed to tend the flock of seven thousand Methodists.

"What a shame if the Methodist societies in America were
to perish!" John cried.

Yet once again, as upset as John may have been over some
colossal external problem, he did not let it slow his other
plans. Healthy again, he started his own periodical in 1777
called *The Arminian Magazine*. Its homeliness he defended:

*It is usual, I am informed, for the compilers
of magazines to employ the outside covers in
acquainting the courteous reader with the
beauties and excellencies. . .therein. I beg
him to excuse me from this trouble. . . .I am
content this magazine should stand or fall by
its own intrinsic value. If it is a compound of
falsehood, ribaldry, and nonsense, let it sink
into oblivion. If it contains only the words of
truth and soberness, then let it meet with a
favorable reception.*

One of the pleasures of the magazine for John was to be
able to publish the emotional poetry of his sister Hetty, dead

189

now for more than twenty-five years but not forgotten.

That same year, amid multitudes who would not stay away because of mere rain, John laid the first stone for a new chapel off City Road. The City Road chapel would replace the Foundry. "The Foundry has been a Methodist center now for nearly forty years!" John said in disbelief. "And now its days are numbered."

The next month, he spoke at a funeral for a young woman. Annoyed that a gentleman and his lady flitted in and out, casual and cool, as if it were a garden party, he blistered them, "Pretty fools! Not for a moment do they realize they will have to account for that folly to God and the angels!" Inside John the fire still burned.

His ire was raised by another incident. William Shent, a wig-maker, had been one of Leeds's first preachers. But he sinned, and in 1778, the society in Leeds expelled him. John was incensed—but not by William Shent. He wrote the society:

> *Who was the occasion of the Methodist preachers first setting foot in Leeds? William Shent.*
>
> *Who received John Nelson into his house at his first coming hither? William Shent.*
>
> *Who was it that stood by me while I preached in the street with stones flying on every side? William Shent.*
>
> *Who was it that bore the storm of persecution for the whole town and stemmed it at the peril of his life? William Shent.*
>
> *Whose word did God bless for many years in an eminent manner? William Shent.*
>
> *By whom were many children now in paradise begotten in the Lord and many now live?*

William Shent.

Who is he that is ready now to be broken up and turned into the street? William Shent.

And does nobody care for this? William Shent fell into sin and was publicly expelled by the Society, but must he be also starved? Must he with gray hairs and all his children be without a place to lay his head? Can you suffer this? . . .Where is gratitude? Where is compassion? Where is Christianity? Where is humanity? . . .You here all arise as one man and roll away the reproach. Let us set him on his feet once more. It may save him and his family. . . .Let it be done quickly. . . .

On the other hand, gratitude for God's protection put him in a joyous mood. He observed with wonder that in forty years he had never been robbed on England's roads, and yet robbery on lonely stretches was common. "Can my safety be due to anything but the hand of God?" he asked.

The war in America seemed almost finished in the fall of 1777. British superiority seemed invincible. But British over-confidence allowed Washington and his badly supplied American army to survive the winter. Britain's old enemy France entered the war in early 1778 to tip the scales. The British were now outnumbered and losing. Sentiment in England was strongly against the war. "Bring the troops back," people clamored. It was rumored Spain soon would join France; then there would be a great European war.

"Let the colonies go!" John said in his private moments.

There was turmoil in City Road chapel now, too. Charles had applied himself diligently to preaching again. He made the City Road chapel his own. He preached there often, and when he didn't, made sure other ordained clergy did. The lay preachers in the circuit were excluded. Charles's critics were quick to point out that sometimes he, now seventy-one, was weak when he preached. But John was pleased to see Charles working hard again, and he knew Charles had earned first rights to preach there. "And although some days Charles is weak, he is still exceptional," John praised.

Other factors tainted Charles for younger Methodists. He lived like a gentleman. He promoted the musical careers of his sons. They held concerts in their home for the high and mighty. Charles was twenty-one and Sammy twelve. They were both prodigies, widely known in London circles as "young Mozarts." This great talent given by God to his sons was Charles's defense against his critics. But the concerts were so refined and proper, even John felt uncomfortable there.

John now was using a coach for travel. He had been thrown by his horse or gone down with his fallen horse dozens of times. But now he was seventy-five, healthy but brittle. His riding days were over. Although Charles would not travel at all, except to visit Bristol by coach occasionally, he nevertheless clopped about London on his old gray horse.

John knew what a debt the Methodists owed Charles. It was no more apparent than in 1780 when he compiled one more hymnal.

Why did the Methodists need yet another hymnal? "Because," John explained in the preface, "the greater part of the people, being poor, are not able to purchase so many books." A new collection of hymns was needed, selected from the other hymnals, and not so large it was not cheap or portable. In the preface, John praised Charles as a true poet. John was terse, analytical. He could have bragged how Handel himself had set six of Charles's hymns to music. What other hymnist could claim such a composer?

Reaction to the new hymnal was immediate. It was regarded as a journey in devotion, a *Pilgrim's Progress* in verse.

The early 1780s were mournful. America was lost; Gen. Cornwallis and his British army were defeated at Yorktown. John's wife Molly died; he did not even get word until after her funeral. Many good friends died: Ebenezer Black-well, Vincent Perronet, Samuel Johnson, James Oglethorpe and John Fletcher. Fletcher, a saintly man with great intellect and drive, had been touted by many as John Wesley's successor.

But John was phenomenally durable. Sometimes John felt God had blessed him with a mission as long-lived as the Apostle John's. At eighty-one, he recorded in his journal:

> *To ease the horses [pulling my coach], we walked from Nairn, ordering Richard [our driver] to follow us, as soon as [the horses] were fed. He did so, but there were two roads. So, as we took one, and he the other, we walked about twelve miles. . .through heavy rain. . . .But blessed be God, I was no more tired than when I set out from Nairn. . . .*

No one seemed more pleased than Charles, who had grown plump. "Everywhere people are amazed by you, John. If they told you what they tell me you would admonish them. 'Oh, what a firm, manly step!' 'Oh, what fresh skin, as clear and smooth as a baby's!' 'Oh, what bright, penetrating eyes!' 'Oh, so that is John Wesley!' You make me envious, brother."

John brushed it off. "Herein is just the same old John Wesley, but with hair as white as almond blossoms," he answered, alluding to a passage in Ecclesiastes on aging.

He had indeed become the venerated old Methodist, even

to the Church of England. Now eighty, after forty-five years of field preaching, he recorded with some satisfaction:

> *I preached at St. Thomas's church in the afternoon, and at St. Swithin's in the evening. The tide is now turned. . . .I have more invitations to preach in churches than I can accept. . . .*

Nevertheless, there was much speculation and anxiety among Methodists about his successor. If something wasn't done formally, the societies might bicker among themselves and just disintegrate after he passed on. And the situation in America neared a crisis. Membership, under the dynamism of Francis Asbury, had swelled to fifteen thousand. But these members needed the sacraments. The Church of England offered no ordained clerics to help. After all, the Church of England reminded John, one of their Thirty-nine Articles swore allegiance to the king! What then were the Methodists of America to do?

In the conference of 1784 at Leeds, John revealed a plan that would shock the Methodists of England—and Charles most of all.

"My scruples are at an end," John said. "Thousands of our American brothers and sisters cannot be baptized nor receive the Holy Communion. For forty years, in my heart I have disagreed with the claim that only the direct succession from the original apostles legitimized Holy Orders. I believe scripturally—and in my heart—that any elder or presbyter in the early church could ordain a minister. And the time has come for me to do likewise."

John proceeded to ordain Thomas Coke the superintendent of the Methodists in America. He wished to avoid the title "bishop," although that was Coke's function. He ordained two more men elders or presbyters. These men were to leave for America and convene a conference as soon as possible.

"Our partnership is dissolved," Charles huffed. "This is preposterous!"

John's next revelation was a plan to manage the societies after he passed on. This conference at Leeds would approve a constitution and set up a "Legal Hundred," the body of leaders who would govern the societies. John still insisted Methodism in England was not a church. He no longer would say that about Methodism in America.

That Christmas, the American Methodists met in Baltimore. They were commissioned by John to form an official church—the Methodist Episcopal Church. Coke was supposed to ordain Asbury the second superintendent of the new church, but Asbury insisted the members vote. Coke and Asbury dutifully were elected not superintendents but bishops. Next, Coke revealed the mountain of material that John Wesley had given him to found the church. Much of it was known, but it now was formalized. Coke unveiled four volumes of John's *Sermons and Notes on the New Testament*, a service *Book of Worship* with liturgies, a *Book of Hymns* and a *Book of Discipline.*

The *Book of Discipline* contained the well-known "General Rules" for Christian conduct. Secondly, it contained the "Articles of Religion." But no longer were there thirty-nine. John had excluded fifteen Church of England articles on hell, creeds, predestination, excommunication and loyalty to the king. A new article swore allegiance to the American government. The resulting twenty-five articles were to become the core of American Methodism.

So although the Methodists in America had established John's Methodism as a church there, Francis Asbury had made it clear they were now independent of John. Meanwhile, in London, John pushed his wiry body on, often courting ruin as he did in January 1785:

> *At this season we usually distribute coals and bread among the poor of the society. But. . . they [needed] clothes, as well as food. So on this, and the four following days I walked through the town, and begged two hundred pounds, in order to clothe them that needed it most. But it was hard work as most of the streets were filled with melting snow, which often lay ankle deep; so that my feet were steeped in snow water nearly from morning till evening. . . .*

He tried to mollify the seething Charles. John kept insisting the Methodist societies in England, Scotland and Ireland would not leave the Church of England. And he kept explaining why Methodism in America had to leave the Church of England. Charles would not agree, bickering with John in a letter:

> *I have been reading over again your "Reasons Against a Separation," printed in 1758. . .and entreat you, in the name of God, and for Christ's sake, to read them again (yourself) . . .and proceed no further. . . .Alas! What trouble are you preparing for yourself, as well as for me, and for your oldest, truest, best friends? . . .*

John was pleased. His brother's threat to leave the Methodists was evaporating. Charles's heat changed to wistful, sorrowful composing:

> *So easily are bishops made,*
> *By man's, or woman's whim.*
> *Wesley his hands on Coke hath laid,*
> *But who laid hands on him?*

Many Methodists thought the 1786 conference at Bristol would see fur fly. Charles himself expected an outcry to separate Methodists from the Church of England because their brothers and sisters in America had separated. But the only thing to upset Charles was a motion to be able to hold society meetings in the same hours the Church of England held services. He cried an angry "No!," but it easily was defeated anyway.

He still seemed to be brooding. Charles was wearing out now. John urged him to get out every day and walk. John himself felt wonderful, although a well-intentioned helper said his writing was become illegible. It certainly did not appear that way to John.

Once again, in January 1787, John took to the streets for five days, soliciting money for the poor. Then he proceeded visiting societies all over the British Isles as he had done for nearly fifty years.

In 1788, Charles passed on—not at all in pain or suffering. He simply did less each day, and one day in March died, at eighty. A poet to the last, he could barely mumble his last verses to his wife Sally, who recorded them:

> *In age and feebleness extreme,*
> *Who shall a sinful worm redeem?*
> *Jesus, my only hope Thou art,*

> *Strength of my failing flesh and heart.*
> *Oh could I catch a smile from Thee*
> *And drop into eternity!*

Charles refused to be buried at City Road chapel as John had suggested. He wished burial in the yard of his Marylbone Church, an official parish of the Church of England.

sixteen

"God is With Us"

Though shaky at the last, the brothers' partnership had endured for almost sixty years. John observed his eighty-fourth birthday in his journal with none of the jubilance of previous years:

> *I am not so agile as I was in times past. I do not run or walk so fast as I did; my sight is a little decayed; my left eye is grown dim, and hardly serves me to read; I have daily some pain in the ball of my right eye, as also in my right temple. . .and in my right shoulder and arm, which I impute partly to a sprain, and partly to rheumatism. I find likewise some decay in my memory, with regard to names and things lately past; but not at all with regard to what I have read or heard twenty, forty, or sixty years ago.*

John's decaying health caused him at last to make a will. He had no money whatever to leave. But who knew how much money might accrue some day from the sale of books? So, optimistic and methodical as ever, he allocated money that might never exist.

"Oh, how I hate to do what I must do next, but I must," he said one day. His deterioration alarmed him so much he felt some very unpleasant tasks he had delayed could be postponed no longer. He was not going to pass on, leaving them for someone else do.

He dismissed his live-in housekeeper at West Street because her husband was a notorious drunk. He turned the reins of his *Arminian Magazine* over to a new editor because his old one made too many mistakes. But both dismissals tore at John's heart.

At the great natural amphitheater in Cornwall late in 1789, his voice was so weak at eighty-six it could not reach his congregation, which numbered twenty-five thousand. On New Year's Day 1790, he wrote:

> *I am now an old man, decayed from head to foot. My eyes are dim; my right hand shakes much; my mouth is hot and dry every morning; I have a lingering fever almost every day; my motion is weak and slow. However, blessed be God, I do not slack my labor. . . .*

He doggedly continued his rounds of the societies. The congregations were enormous. It was obvious to John why: they did not expect to see him again. This was farewell.

As he made his rounds, he marveled at what was happening in England. Factories were springing up wherever there was plenty of water and coal. It seemed new machines were invented daily. Steel rolling, the cotton-spinning jenny, the steam engine. The war with America was forgotten. This seemed a new era for Britain where the common man would find plenty of work making cotton cloth and steel and machinery.

"Whether this age of machinery will be good or not I do not know," he admitted, "but God certainly placed our societies in these blossoming giants: Leeds, Manchester, Birmingham and Sheffield."

He hardly dared think what he had done in fifty years. In years past, he had ignored such retrospect; there had been too much yet to do. But now the end was near. He could indulge a little in memories. He had traveled at least two hundred thousand miles on sea and land. He had preached more than forty thousand sermons. And how many times had he traveled his triangle of Methodist centers in London, Bristol and Newcastle? Fifty times? No, more. Beyond the triangle to places like Canterbury and Cornwall? Forty times? And how many passages across the sea to Ireland? Twenty-one, was it? And how much time spent in Ireland in all? Five years? And how many Methodists were there now worldwide? Fifty thousand? And righteous, too.

He would leave the church a thought or two as to organization. Yes, one must evangelize. But the babe in Christ then must be brought into the fold, too. The class meeting was a wonder. There, God's children practiced holiness, learned discipline, and reached into their pockets to help the poor. His societies had extended the Church of England into a social machine as efficient as any machine of steel in the new industrial revolution.

Then there was the church he had founded. Yes, he, the John Wesley who had pledged everlasting loyalty to the Church of England, had founded a church. In the realm of his greatest failure blossomed the American Methodist Episcopal Church. By all accounts it was a vibrant church, led by tireless Francis Asbury. Asbury, some said, was going to outride, outpreach and outdo John himself. "If God wills it," John thought, "then that is good. Praise God."

And what of his beloved England? There were those who said England would have seen a revolt like that in France had not John Wesley attended the masses. Well, if it was true, John was pleased, but the glory was God's. Some said his scathing opposition to slavery had encouraged some in Parliament like William Wilberforce to try to abolish it, and its abolition in England was not far off. Well, if it was true, John was pleased, but the glory was God's.

In October 1790, he no longer could write in his journal. He needed constant companions now, helping him in every way. Sister Betsy Ritchie rarely left his side.

Friday, February 25, 1791, after a morning visit to friends, he returned to his apartment in the City Road center extremely tired. He went to his bedroom right away and there became sick. He was feverish. He had never felt so tired.

It was the next day before he realized it. He seemed in constant sleep. His doctor was there now.

Sunday he felt better. He at least could take broth. There was talk of another physician. "I am perfectly satisfied with my physician and will not have anyone else," John said forcefully.

The hours passed drowsily. A sharp pain in his chest startled him, but it faded. Soon he heard someone say it was Tuesday. Where was Monday? How many times in the past had he chosen to ignore some ailment and then miraculously God had removed it? He sang praise to God:

> *All glory to God in the sky,*
> *And peace upon earth be restored.*

But his strength quickly failed him. This singing was not God's will.

"Bring me a pen and ink," he whispered. He would write his praise. God must be praised. But when he held the pen on paper, nothing happened. He could not coordinate his hand. He tried again later. Nothing. It was not God's will.

"Let me write for you, sir," Betsy offered. "Tell me what you would say."

"Nothing, but that God is with us." John didn't explain it meant nothing to have someone else write his praise. The praise had to be his.

Later he tried to rise. He couldn't. How often had he seen the dying unable to do anything but sing praise? He would sing again. Surely God would let him. John sang:

> *I'll praise my Maker while I've breath,*
> *And when my voice is lost in death,*
> *Praise shall employ my nobler pow'rs;*
> *My days of praise shall ne'er be past,*
> *While life, and thought, and being last,*
> *Or immortality endures.*

He tried to rise again. Many hands raised him. He was taken to his chair. He felt very weak, but this time he was not sleepy.

In a weak voice, he said, "Lord, Thou givest strength to those who can speak, and to those who cannot. Speak, Lord, to all our hearts, and let them know that Thou loosest tongues." And he sang a line or two.

But then he was silent. He knew now every exertion brought him closer to the end. He had some final business. In whispers, he told of the contents of his bureau and the location of its key. He requested to be buried in something woolen. He asked that the sermon he had written on the love of God be widely distributed.

Was there anything else? He must reassure the others. It seemed a long time before he sputtered weakly, "The best of all is, God is with us."

There was nothing to do now but praise God. To die is gain. Psalm 46 floated through his mind again and again:

> *God is our refuge and strength,*
> *An ever-present help in trouble.*
> *Therefore we will not fear,*
> *Though the earth give way,*
> *And the mountains fall*
> *Into the heart of the sea;*
> *Though its waters roar and foam,*
> *And the mountains quake with their surging.*

Though the world turns upside down, John thought, *God is there. Praise Him:*

> *There is a river whose streams*
> *Make glad the city of God,*
> *The holy place where the Most High dwells.*
> *God is within her, she will not fall;*
> *God will help her at break of day.*
> *Nations are in uproar, kingdoms fall;*
> *He lifts his voice, the earth melts.*

Oh, John thought, *the world ends.* And at last begins the precious City of God this pilgrim has longed for.

> *The Lord Almighty is with us;*
> *The God of Jacob is our fortress.*

Oh, yes, praise God, our stronghold, our citadel, our castle, John thought.

> *Come and see the works of the Lord,*

The desolations He has brought on the earth.
He makes wars cease to the ends of the earth;
He breaks the bow and shatters the spear,
He burns the shields with fire.
"Be still, and know that I am God;
I will be exalted among the nations,
I will be exalted in the earth."

Oh, yes, God will still the earth, John thought. *Praise Him.*

The Lord Almighty is with us;
The God of Jacob is our fortress.

Amen. Oh, praise God, our stronghold, John thought.

The room was dark now. He heard words—no, phrases of the same psalm. Was it his own voice? Or was the room abounding, swelling in praise?

The room became light again. Was it another day? Or was it ministering spirits? There were vague obelisks around his bed. Friends? Murmuring. Voices? He tried to move. He could not. He tried to speak. Did he say "farewell?" Perhaps. It was done then. Praise God.

Further Reading on John Wesley

I. Biographies of John Wesley:

Brailsfore, Mabel R., *A Tale of Two Brothers: John & Charles Wesley*. New York: Oxford University Press, 1954. More Charles than John, but excellent.

Church, L.F., *Knight of the Burning Hearts: the Story of John Wesley*. New York: Abingdon-Cokesbury Press, 1952. Artful and entertaining storytelling.

Ethridge, Willie Snow, *Strange Fires*. New York: Vanguard Press, 1971. His bizarre 'courtship' in Georgia.

Green, V.H.H., *Young Mr. Wesley*. New York: St. Martin's Press, 1961. Through his Oxford days. Scholarly.

Lee, Umphrey, *The Lord's Horseman*. New York: Abingdom Press, 1928. Scholarly, entertaining assessment.

II. Compilations of John Wesley's writings include:

Wesley, John (ed. Percy L. Parker),*The Heart of John Wesley's Journal*. New York: Fleming H. Revell Company, 1902. Standard introduction to Wesley.

Wesley, John (ed. Nehemiah Curnock), *The Journal of the Reverend John Wesley*, 8 Vols. London: Epworth Press, 1938.

Wesley, John (ed. John Telford), *Letters of Reverend John Wesley*, 8 Vols. London: Epworth Press, 1931.

Wesley, John (ed. Frederick C. Gill), *Selected Letters*. New York: The Philosophical Library, 1956.

HEROES OF THE FAITH

This exciting biographical series explores the lives of famous Christian men and women throughout the ages. These trade paper books will inspire and encourage you to follow the example of these "Heroes of the Faith" who made Christ the center of their existence. 208 pages each. Only $3.97 each!

Available wherever books are sold.

Or order from:
Barbour Publishing, Inc.
P.O. Box 719
Uhrichsville, Ohio 44683
http://www.barbourbooks.com

If you order by mail, add $2.00 to your order for shipping.
Prices subject to change without notice.